First World War
and Army of Occupation
War Diary
France, Belgium and Germany

16 DIVISION
48 Infantry Brigade
Royal Irish Rifles
7th Battalion
19 December 1915 - 15 November 1917

WO95/1975/2

The Naval & Military Press Ltd
www.nmarchive.com
Published in association with The National Archives

Published by

The Naval & Military Press Ltd

Unit 10 Ridgewood Industrial Park,

Uckfield, East Sussex,

TN22 5QE England

Tel: +44 (0) 1825 749494

www.naval-military-press.com

www.nmarchive.com

This diary has been reprinted in facsimile from the original. Any imperfections are inevitably reproduced and the quality may fall short of modern type and cartographic standards.

© **Crown Copyright**
Images reproduced by permission of The National Archives, London, England, 2015.

Contents

Document type	Place/Title	Date From	Date To
Heading	1975/2 1915 Dec-1917 Nov 7 Battalion Royal Irish Fusiliers		
Heading	16th Division 49th Infy Bde 7th Bn Roy. Irish Rifles 1917 Aug & Sep		
Heading	Dec 15 Jly 17 19/12/15-30/6/16 7th R. Irish Rifles Vol. 1 18-31 Dec		
War Diary	Blackdown	19/12/1915	20/12/1915
War Diary	Havre	20/12/1915	21/12/1915
War Diary	Noeux-Les Mines	22/12/1915	28/12/1915
War Diary	Philosophe	29/12/1915	29/12/1915
War Diary	Noeux-Les Mines	30/12/1915	09/01/1916
War Diary	Hesdigneul ref 1/40.000 Sheet 36 B	01/02/1916	29/02/1916
War Diary	Ham-En Artois	01/03/1916	31/03/1916
War Diary	Trenches	01/04/1916	03/04/1916
War Diary	Philosophe	04/04/1916	30/04/1916
War Diary	Trenches	17/04/1916	31/05/1916
War Diary	Noeux-Les-Mines	01/06/1916	30/06/1916
Miscellaneous	Report "A"	27/06/1916	27/06/1916
Miscellaneous	Report "B"	28/06/1916	28/06/1916
Heading	July 1916		
Heading	War Diary 7th (S) Bn The Royal Irish Rifles 1st. July To 31st July 1916 Volume No. 8		
War Diary	In The Field	01/07/1916	09/07/1916
War Diary	Trenches	10/07/1916	11/07/1916
War Diary	Noeux	11/07/1916	19/07/1916
War Diary	Trenches	19/07/1916	21/07/1916
War Diary	Mazingarbe	23/07/1916	23/07/1916
War Diary	Trenches	24/07/1916	01/08/1916
Heading	War Diary 7th Royal Irish Rifles Month Of August, 1916 Volume 9		
War Diary	Trenches	01/08/1916	12/08/1916
War Diary	Philosophe	12/08/1916	12/08/1916
War Diary	Trenches	16/08/1916	24/08/1916
War Diary	Allouagne	25/08/1916	26/08/1916
War Diary	Corbie	30/08/1916	30/08/1916
War Diary	Sandpit She 62 D N.E. E 193	31/08/1916	31/08/1916
Heading	Sept 1916		
Miscellaneous	D.A.G. 3rd Echelon Base	01/10/1916	01/10/1916
War Diary	Sandpit Sheet 62 D NE	01/09/1916	01/09/1916
War Diary	Billon Farm	03/09/1916	03/09/1916
War Diary	Carnoy	03/09/1916	03/09/1916
War Diary	Bernafay Wood	04/09/1916	04/09/1916
War Diary	Guillemont	04/09/1916	06/09/1916
War Diary	Front Line	07/09/1916	08/09/1916
War Diary	Front Line W of Ginchy	08/09/1916	08/09/1916
War Diary	Ginchy	09/09/1916	10/09/1916
War Diary	Happy Valley	10/09/1916	10/09/1916
War Diary	Corbie	11/09/1916	15/09/1916
War Diary	Ginchy	09/09/1916	09/09/1916
War Diary	Longpre	18/09/1916	18/09/1916

War Diary	Laclytte	21/09/1916	21/09/1916
War Diary	Trenches	23/09/1916	30/09/1916
Heading	War Diary Month Of October, 1916 Volume 11 7th Royal Irish Rifles		
War Diary	Sheet 28 S.W. Klondyke Farm	01/10/1916	01/10/1916
War Diary	Trenches	05/10/1916	13/10/1916
War Diary	Locre	14/10/1916	21/10/1916
War Diary	Trenches	21/10/1916	31/10/1916
Heading	War Diary For Month Of November, 1916 Volume 12 7th Ro. Irish Rifles		
War Diary	Sheet 28 SW 1820,000 Kemmel	01/11/1916	05/11/1916
War Diary	Trenches	06/11/1916	16/11/1916
War Diary	Locre	17/11/1916	21/11/1916
War Diary	Sheet 28 1/20,000	21/11/1916	21/11/1916
War Diary	Trenches	22/11/1916	28/11/1916
War Diary	Kemmel	29/11/1916	30/11/1916
Heading	War Diary For Month Of December, 1916 Volume 13 7th Ro. Irish Rifles		
War Diary	Kemmel	01/12/1916	04/12/1916
War Diary	Trenches	05/12/1916	10/12/1916
War Diary	Locre	11/12/1916	17/12/1916
War Diary	Trenches	17/12/1916	22/12/1916
War Diary	Kemmel	23/12/1916	27/12/1916
War Diary	Trenches	28/12/1916	31/12/1916
Heading	War Diary for month of January, 1917 Volume 14 7th Royal Irish Rifles		
War Diary	Trenches	01/01/1917	09/01/1917
War Diary	Sheet 20/SW 1/20000	10/01/1917	11/01/1917
War Diary	Trenches	12/01/1917	31/01/1917
Heading	War Diary For Month Of February, 1917 Volume 15 Unit:- 7th Royal Irish Rifles		
War Diary	Trenches	01/02/1917	05/02/1917
War Diary	Locre	06/02/1917	12/02/1917
War Diary	Trenches	13/02/1917	21/02/1917
War Diary	Butterfly Farm	22/02/1917	28/02/1917
Heading	War Diary For Month Of March, 1917 Volume 16 Unit:- 7th Royal Irish Rifles		
War Diary	Trenches	01/03/1917	14/03/1917
War Diary	Locre	15/03/1917	29/03/1917
War Diary	Hazebrouck	31/03/1917	31/03/1917
Heading	War Diary For Month Of April, 1917 Volume:- 17 Unit:- 7th R. Irish Rifles		
War Diary	Hallines	01/04/1917	01/04/1917
War Diary	Tournehem	02/04/1917	14/04/1917
War Diary	Locre	15/04/1917	18/04/1917
War Diary	Trenches	19/04/1917	26/04/1917
War Diary	Rossignol Estaminet	27/04/1917	30/04/1917
Heading	War Diary Volume 18 For Month Of May, 1917 Unit:- 7th R. Irish Rifles		
War Diary	Rossignol Estaminet	01/05/1917	03/05/1917
War Diary	Dezon Camp	05/05/1917	08/05/1917
War Diary	Kennel Shelters near Kemmel	09/05/1917	10/05/1917
War Diary	Birr Barracks	11/05/1917	18/05/1917
War Diary	Trenches	18/05/1917	25/05/1917
Map	Creeping Barrage Map		
War Diary	Butterfly Farm	26/05/1917	31/05/1917

Heading	War Diary For Month Of June, 1917 Volume:- 19 Unit:- 7th (S) Battle Royal Irish Rifles		
War Diary	Butterfly Farm	01/06/1917	01/06/1917
War Diary	Clare Camp	02/06/1917	06/06/1917
War Diary	Opposite Wytschaete	07/06/1917	11/06/1917
War Diary	Clare Camp	12/06/1917	12/06/1917
War Diary	On March	13/06/1917	13/06/1917
War Diary	Rouge Croix	14/06/1917	16/06/1917
War Diary	On March	17/06/1917	18/06/1917
War Diary	Croix Rouge	19/06/1917	19/06/1917
War Diary	On March	20/06/1917	20/06/1917
War Diary	Steenvoorde	21/06/1917	21/06/1917
War Diary	On March.	22/06/1917	22/06/1917
War Diary	Rubrouck	23/06/1917	30/06/1917
Miscellaneous	7th (S) Bn Royal Irish Rifles Order No 118	06/06/1917	06/06/1917
Miscellaneous	7th (S) Bn Royal Irish Rifles Provisional Operation Instructions	05/06/1917	05/06/1917
Heading	War Diary For Month Of July, 1917 Volume:- 20 Unit:- 7th (S) Bn Royal Irish Rifles		
War Diary	Rubrouck	01/07/1917	09/07/1917
War Diary	Cormette	10/07/1917	16/07/1917
War Diary	Zaggers Cappel	17/07/1917	21/07/1917
War Diary	Camp Wimezeele	22/07/1917	24/07/1917
War Diary	Camp Watou Area No 1	25/07/1917	29/07/1917
War Diary	Toronto Camp G18a 5.7	30/07/1917	30/07/1917
War Diary	Trenches	31/07/1917	31/07/1917
Miscellaneous	7th (S) Bn Royal Irish Rifles. Order No 124	07/07/1917	07/07/1917
Miscellaneous	7th (S) Bn Royal Irish Rifles. Order No 143	10/07/1917	10/07/1917
Miscellaneous	7th (S) Bn Royal Irish Rifles. Order No 125	13/07/1917	13/07/1917
Miscellaneous	7th (S) Bn Royal Irish Rifles. Order No 125	15/07/1917	15/07/1917
Miscellaneous	7th (S) Bn Royal Irish Rifles Order No 127	21/07/1917	21/07/1917
Miscellaneous	7th (S) Bn Royal Irish Rifles Order No 128	24/07/1917	24/07/1917
Miscellaneous	7th (S) Bn Royal Irish Rifles Order No 129	30/07/1917	30/07/1917
Heading	War Diary For Month Of August, 1917 Volume 21 Unit 7th Royal Irish Rifles		
War Diary	Trenches	01/08/1917	01/08/1917
War Diary	Toronto Camp G 18a5.7	02/08/1917	04/08/1917
War Diary	Ecole Ypres	05/08/1917	06/08/1917
War Diary	Freezen Berg	07/08/1917	09/08/1917
War Diary	Camp Of H15b4.8	10/08/1917	10/08/1917
War Diary	Viamertinghe	10/08/1917	14/08/1917
War Diary	Trenches	15/08/1917	17/08/1917
War Diary	Near Poperinghe	18/08/1917	19/08/1917
War Diary	Wormhoudt	20/08/1917	20/08/1917
War Diary	Courcelles Le Compte	21/08/1917	22/08/1917
War Diary	Achiet-Le-Petit	23/08/1917	27/08/1917
War Diary	No 9 Camp Near Ervillers	28/08/1917	31/08/1917
Operation(al) Order(s)	7th (S) Bn Royal Irish Rifles. Order No 132	05/08/1917	05/08/1917
Operation(al) Order(s)	7th (S) Bn Royal Irish Rifles. Order No 133	14/08/1917	14/08/1917
Operation(al) Order(s)	7th (S) Bn Royal Irish Rifles. Order No 134	15/08/1917	15/08/1917
Operation(al) Order(s)	7th (S) Bn Royal Irish Rifles. Order No 135	27/08/1917	27/08/1917
Operation(al) Order(s)	7/8th. (S) Battalion The Royal Irish Fusiliers Order No. 21	27/08/1917	27/08/1917
Operation(al) Order(s)	7/8th. (S) Battalion The Royal Irish Fusiliers Order No. 21	21/08/1917	21/08/1917

Map	Trenches Corrected From Information Received Up To 22.7.17		
Miscellaneous			
Heading	War Diary For Month Of September, 1917 Volume 22 Unit:- 7th Btn R. Irish Rifles		
War Diary	Ervillers	01/09/1917	03/09/1917
War Diary	Trenches	04/09/1917	10/09/1917
War Diary	Sheet 51B 1/40000	11/09/1917	14/09/1917
War Diary	Trenches	15/09/1917	16/09/1917
War Diary	Ervillers	17/09/1917	27/09/1917
War Diary	Trenches	28/09/1917	30/09/1917
Operation(al) Order(s)	7th (S) Bn Royal Irish Rifles. Orders No 136	03/09/1917	03/09/1917
Operation(al) Order(s)	7th (S) Bn Royal Irish Rifles. Orders No 137	09/09/1917	09/09/1917
Miscellaneous			
Operation(al) Order(s)	7th (S) Bn Royal Irish Rifles Order No 136	15/09/1917	15/09/1917
Miscellaneous	Move to after relief		
Operation(al) Order(s)	7th (Service) Battalion Royal Irish Rifles Operation Order No. 139		
Heading	36th Division 108th Infy Bde 7th Bn Roy. Irish Rif. Oct-Nov 1917		
War Diary	Trenches 51B SW 1820,000	01/10/1917	09/10/1917
War Diary	Ervillers	10/10/1917	15/10/1917
War Diary	Ytres	16/10/1917	31/10/1917
Operation(al) Order(s)	Order No. 140 By Lieut Col S.G. Francis D.S.O. Commanding 7th (Service) Battn Royal Irish Rifles.	03/10/1917	03/10/1917
Operation(al) Order(s)	Order No. 141 By Lieut Col S.G. Francis D.S.O. Commanding 7th (Service) Battn Royal Irish Rifles.	09/10/1917	09/10/1917
Miscellaneous	Table Of Reliefs		
War Diary	Ytres	01/11/1917	15/11/1917

1975/2
1915 Dec – 1917 Nov
7 Battalion Royal Irish Fusiliers

Attached { 16TH DIVISION
49TH INFY BDE

7TH BN ROY. IRISH RIFLES
~~AUG 1917 ONLY~~
1917 Aug & Sep

48/16.

7th R. Irish Rifles
Vol. I
15 - 31 Dec

16

Dec 15
Jly '17
19/12/15 - 30/6/16

Army Form C. 2118.

WAR DIARY
or
INTELLIGENCE SUMMARY
(Erase heading not required.)

Instructions regarding War Diaries and Intelligence Summaries are contained in F. S. Regs., Part II. and the Staff Manual respectively. Title pages will be prepared in manuscript.

Place	Date	Hour	Summary of Events and Information	Remarks and references to Appendices
Blackdown	19/11/15	4-30 am	Left Blackdown and entrained for SOUTHAMPTON. Embarked 4-30 pm	16
BLACKDOWN	20/11/15		and arrived at HAVRE 7-30 a.m. marched to Rest Camp.	16
HAVRE	20/11/15	8-0 pm	Entrained at HAVRE.	16
	21/11/15	4-30 pm	Arrived at FOUGEREUIL. A & B Coys marched to NŒUX-LES-MINES C & D Coys marched to HOUCHIN	16
NŒUX-LES-MINES	22/11/15 23/11/15		In Camp.	16
	24/11/15		Commanding Officer & Adjutant proceeded to PHILOSOPHE attached to Sussex Regt. in trenches.	16
	25/11/15 26/11/15		C.O. & Adjt. returned to trenches. Remainder of Battalion in Camp at NŒUX-LES-MINES and HOUCHIN.	16 16

Army Form C. 2118.

WAR DIARY
or
INTELLIGENCE SUMMARY.
(Erase heading not required.)

Instructions regarding War Diaries and Intelligence
Summaries are contained in F. S. Regs., Part II.
and the Staff Manual respectively. Title pages
will be prepared in manuscript.

Place	Date	Hour	Summary of Events and Information	Remarks and references to Appendices
Nœux les Mines	27/11/17		C.O. & Adjr. Returned to NŒUX-LES-MINES. Remainder of Battalion in Camp.	16
	28/11/17		In Camp.	16
PHILOSOPHE	29/11/17		A & B Coys moved to PHILOSOPHE & took up position in old British line. South of WING'S Way. Platoons 1, 2, 5 and 6 near its support line.	16
	30/11/17		A & B Coys remained as for 29th. C & D Coy moves. We Relieved at NŒUX-LES-MINES.	16
NŒUX-LES-MINES	31/11/17		Platoons 9, 10, 13 & 14 went into old British line. 3, 4, 7, 8 & its support line. 1, 2, 5 & 6 in firing line.	

WAR DIARY
INTELLIGENCE SUMMARY

Army Form C. 2118.

Place	Date	Hour	Summary of Events and Information	Remarks and references to Appendices
	10/1/16.		B.D. HDqrs, A&B Coys, 9.10.13 & Horses at A.M.E.S. 11-12. 15076 Horses marched from NOEUX-LES-MINES to A.M.E.S.	16.
	11/1/16 Tues		At A.M.E.S. Bn. Training. Close order Squadron. A&B Coys. Fired Extraction on range. D.S.O.	16.
	28/1/16		Brigadier-General Ramsay. General Armed J. & 8" INF RDE on 2.3." 2 Officers sent to 47" Div. Bombing School - LABEUVRIÈRE. 3 " " " " " FERFAY. 1 " " " " " LA.RE.S. 1 " " " " " LA.RE.S. 16 "Div. Young Officers Course LAIRE.S.	
	28/1/6.		Major. A.G. Francis. D.S.O. assumed Comd of station. Batt. moved to found billets at HESDIGNEUL.	16.
	28/31		At HESDIGNEUL.	16.

Signed AGFrancis Major
Cmdg 7 Royal Irish Rifles
31-1-16

Army Form C. 2118.

WAR DIARY
or
INTELLIGENCE SUMMARY.
(Erase heading not required.)

Instructions regarding War Diaries and Intelligence Summaries are contained in F. S. Regs., Part II. and the Staff Manual respectively. Title pages will be prepared in manuscript.

Place	Date	Hour	Summary of Events and Information	Remarks and references to Appendices
NOEUX-LES-MINES.	1/1/16	—	All A & B Coys and 9.10.13 of 14 Platoons in trenches — latter four in old British line. Lieut. T.P. FARRELLY — Transport Officer — wounded on HULLUCH road while taking up rations — four wounded in other ranks — four wounded.	96.
	2/1/16		11.12. 15 & 16 Platoons left NOEUX-LES-MINES and proceeded to old British line (attacked 1st Div.) 1-2. 5 & 6 Platoons left trenches and returned to billets at NOEUX-LES-MINES.	96.
	3/1/16		1.2.5 & 6 Platoons and B.H. Hdqrs at NOEUX-LES-MINES.	96.
	4/1/16	9.0 a.m.	1.2.5.6 Platoons left NOEUX-LES-MINES and proceeded to trenches billets at AMETTES. 3.4. 7-8 Platoons left trenches and returned to billets at NOEUX-LES-MINES. Do for 4th.	96.
	5/1/16		B.H. Hdqrs and 3.4.7 & 8 Platoons returned forwards to billets at AMETTES.	96.
	6/1/16		9.10.13 & 14 Platoons returned from trenches to NOEUX-LES-MINES.	4.
	7/1/16		Do for 6th.	
	8/1/16		B.H. Hdqrs and A & B Coys moved from AMETTES to AMETTES. Rev billets at AMETTES. 9.10.12 & 14 Platoons forward from NOEUX-LES-MINES to AMETTES. 16th Divl. HQrs took 11-12. 15 & 16 Platoons returned to NOEUX-LES-MINES from trenches.	26.
	9/1/16		Do for 8th.	16.

Army Form C. 2118.

WAR DIARY
or
INTELLIGENCE SUMMARY.
(Erase heading not required.)

Instructions regarding War Diaries and Intelligence Summaries are contained in F.S. Regs., Part II. and the Staff Manual respectively. Title pages will be prepared in manuscript.

Place	Date	Hour	Summary of Events and Information	Remarks and references to Appendices
HESDIGNEUL v/s L.O.O.O Sheet 36.B.	1/2/16		Machine Gun Section under Lieut. J.S. STEELE proceed to MAZINGARBE and was attached to 46th Inf. Bde. Remainder of Batt" at HESDIGNEUL.	96.
	2/2/16 till 8/2/16		Bat" remained at HESDIGNEUL attached to IV"th Corps. Working parties supplied daily at AUCHEL.	96.
			HESDIGNEUL and MINK. Except on 14th and 16th.	
	12/2/16		2 Lt L.B. HIBBS relieved Lt. STEELE with Machine Gun Section	96.
	13/2/16		Machine Gun Section relieved by Section of 9th R. MUNSTER Fus.	96.
	14/2/16		Machine Gun Section returned to HESDIGNEUL	96.
	19/2/16		Battalion moved to SAILLY LABOURSE – attached to 12th Div – 1st Corps.	96.
	19/2/16		Companies proceeded to trenches and were attached separately to battalions of 36th Bde.	96.
			Headquarters remained at SAILLY LABOURSE. Ref 20.000 Sheet 36.C. G4, G5.	96.
	20/2/16	5-30pm	1 O.R. killed, 3 O.R. wounded by grenades in front line trench.	96.
	22/2/16		Companies returned to Billets in SAILLY LABOURSE	96.
	23/2/16		Remained in Billets at SAILLY LABOURSE	96.
	24/2/16	2.0 pm	Battalion relieved 6th ROYAL WEST KENTS (37th Bde 40E) in trenches, taking over line from KAISERIN TRENCH to MUDTRENCH. Ref. 36.C. NORTH. from B.2. to G.4 d 7.6 to A.2.8 c.3.3.	96.
	25/2/16	12 noon	2 men of 2.3rd BAVARIAN Regt. – went on a patrol surrendered at A.2.8.c.4.1. One spoke English. They were handed over to A.P.M. 12th Div. on morning of 26/2/16.	96.

WAR DIARY
or
INTELLIGENCE SUMMARY.
(Erase heading not required.)

Army Form C. 2118.

Place	Date	Hour	Summary of Events and Information	Remarks and references to Appendices
	26/9/16		Remained in trenches. Casualties :- 1 Sergeant - attacked from 6th R.W. KENTS - killed by r/g grenade. 1 man slightly wounded by sniper bullet.	16
	27/9/16		Lieut CLIFF McCULLOCH M.A. killed. Capt T.J. DOBSON wounded. 5 O.R. wounded by rifle grenade. Battalion relieved by 6th ROYAL WEST KENTS - relief commencing at 2 p.m. and being completed at 4-30 p.m. Returned to billets at SAILLY LABOURSE. VERMELLES was shelled by enemy artillery while battalion was passing through. 10 O.R. wounded by shell. During this time in the trenches there were no operations initiated either by us or The enemy with the exception of activity on both sides with rifle grenades and Trench mortars. Our machine gunners displayed revealed nothing further. We suffered working parties. Great portion of KAISER N. TRENCH and SAVILLE ROW the R.E. throughout the two days on trip rapo. Great junction of GUILFORD TRENCH and STICKY TRENCH. the site at the junction of	16 16 16 16
	28/9/16 29/9/16		marched to billets in 48th INF BDE area at HAM-EN-ARTOIS. Remained in billets at HAM-EN-ARTOIS.	16.

M. Arnez 2nd Lieut H.Q's
Capt.

7R 1+ R f

Army Form C. 2118.

WAR DIARY
or
INTELLIGENCE SUMMARY
(Erase heading not required.)

Instructions regarding War Diaries and Intelligence Summaries are contained in F. S. Regs., Part II. and the Staff Manual respectively. Title pages will be prepared in manuscript.

Place	Date	Hour	Summary of Events and Information	Remarks and references to Appendices
HAM-EN ARTOIS	1/3/16 to 8/3/16		Remained in billets at HAM-EN-ARTOIS. Ref sheet 36 A. Square O.24.c.	96.
	9/3/16		Draft of 1 Sergt, 1 Corporal and 26 men from 5th Batt arrived on 5th march.	8.
	9/3/16		Marched to billets in 1st Corps res Reserve Area at LAPUGNOY. Ref sheet 36 B Square 16.	96.
	10/3/16 11/3/16 12/3/16		Remained in billets at LAPUGNOY	✓.
	13/3/16		"A" Coy proceeded for attachment to 16th Div. School at LABEUVRIERE. Ref Sheet 36 B. S.D.1.9.a.	96.
	14/3/16		In billets at LAPUGNOY. Remainder. "A" Coy at LABEUVRIERE	96.
	21/3/16		2nd Lieut L.B. HIBBS died in 18 Casualty Clearing Station.	96.
	22/3/16		Advance Party proceeded to trenches. Battn relieved HULLUCH SECTION relf battalion left Brigade.	96.
	23/3/16		2nd Advance Party proceeded 15 butchers as above.	9.
	24/3/16		Batt: entrained at LAPUGNOY – proceeded to NOEUX-LES-MINES – marched to trenches at 10h over centre at section of HULLUCH SECTION from 4th K.O.S.B. At 6·20 pm the enemy exploded two mines opposite the Welsh NORTHERN and SOUTHERN S.A.P. On our line Guns and men were buried. Our other three guns – under command of L/Gt BARNETT – promptly opened fire and prevented the enemy from occupying the lips of the craters. Casualties. 2.O.R. killed. 2.O.R. wounded.	96.

#353 Wt. W2544/1454 700,000 5/15 D.D.&L. A.D.S.S./Forms/C. 2118.

WAR DIARY
or
INTELLIGENCE SUMMARY.

(Erase heading not required.)

Army Form C. 2118.

Place	Date	Hour	Summary of Events and Information	Remarks and references to Appendices
	27/7/16		In trenches. Casualties from r/g grenades and trench mortars. 7 O.R. killed. 4 O.R. wounded	do.
	28/7/16		A & C Coys relieved by 9th MUNSTERS and 8th DUBLINS. D Coy remained in reserve line. HQrs and M.G.C. Coys 15 PHILOSOPHÉ in Bde Reserve. M.G. section remained in line. 1 O.R. wounded	do.
	29/7/16		As for 28th. 1 O.R. M.Gp killed by rifle grenade. 1 O.R. D. Coy wounded	do.
	30/7/16		Brigade now holding section with two battalions in front line. battalion HQrs in half section from 9th MUNSTERS. A Coy HOLLY LANE to HATTERLEY SOUTHERN SAP (inclusive) B Coy SOUTHERN SAP to KING'S WAY. C Coy KING'S WAY ESTON STREET.	do.
	31/7/16		D Coy in support. Ais for 30th. Enemy active about 1 am with trench mortars & Rifle Grenades	do.

Commander 7 (S) Batt. Royal Irish Rifles

J. Craigher Adjt
for Lt. Col.

Army Form C. 2118.

WAR DIARY
or
INTELLIGENCE SUMMARY.

Page 2.

7th (S) Bn. R¹ Irish Rifles.

(Erase heading not required.)

Place	Date	Hour	Summary of Events and Information	Remarks and references to Appendices
Bailes	1/4/16	6.6 pm	We exploded a small mine just South of junction of A SIXTH AVENUE and firing line at 10 pm.	16.
	2/4/16		Our artillery bombard the enemy's front line from 10.0 pm till 10.10 pm. Casualties. Capt. G.M. JOHNSTON kills. 2/Lt. J.W. DICKSON wounds.	16.
			Draft of 1 officer and 58 O.R. joined battalion. (Officer – 2/Lt EATON – from 19th Batt¹).	16.
	3/4/16		Relieved by 9th MUNSTERS. Proceed to billets (at 2 hours notice).	16.
PHILOSOPHE	4/4/16 5/4/16		In billets at PHILOSOPHE.	16.
	6/4/16 morn		Relieved by 7th LEINSTERS. Proceed to billets in NOEUX-LES-MINES (at 2 hours notice).	16.
	6/12 6/10		In billets at NOEUX-LES-MINES.	16.
	11/4/16		Relieved 8th R. Sc. Fusiliers (49th Inf Bde.) in Right sub-section of Pu its 14 bis section. Relief	16.
	13/4/16		complete at 12.35 am. 13/4/16. B. C & D Coys in front and support lines. A Coy in Reserve trench.	16.
	15/4/16		In trenches. NORTHERN PYLON of LOOS TOWERS knocked down by enemy shell fire at 2-15 pm	16.
	14/4/16.		In trenches. Draft of 4 O.R. joined batt.. 1/Lt J.F. ROWLANDS rejoined battalion from hospital	16.
	15/4/16		Remaining PYLON of LOOS TOWERS knocked down by enemy artillery at 3.30 pm. Battalion relieved by	16.
	16/4/16.		9th MUNSTERS and took up new position in Brigade Support. One Company in GUN TRENCH, one platoon in 65 metre redoubt, 2 coys & exp. & 2 coys & platoon in NORTHERN SAP & platoon in TENTH AVENUE.	11.

Army Form C. 2118.

WAR DIARY or **INTELLIGENCE SUMMARY.**
XVI   7/h (S) Bn. Royal Irish Rifle Vol 5
(Erase heading not required.)

Instructions regarding War Diaries and Intelligence Summaries are contained in F. S. Regs., Part II. and the Staff Manual respectively. Title pages will be prepared in manuscript.

Place	Date	Hour	Summary of Events and Information	Remarks and references to Appendices
1st 4th Trenches	17/4/16 18/4/16 19/4/16	—	Working parties supplied daily to R.E. and pioneers.	96.
"	20/4/16		Relieved 9th MUNSTERS in Right 2nd section. Quiet in his section. 20.R wounded still. One man 9/5S2 Regiment shortly one from sentries at 4 a.m.	96.
	21/4/16		S.O.R. killed and 9.O.R wounded. – shell –	12.
	22/4/16 23/4/16		4/U. S. CEATON wounded. Capt. S.B. MASSEY joined battalion from 5th in batt. Lt. C.A.O.G.I.S.R wounded.	96. 96.
	24/4/16		Relieved by 9th Munsters. Brigade Reserve in PHILOSOPHE.	96.
	25/4/16	5.00 am	Enemy set bore go from Quib 14 bn follows by a heavy bombardment. Then attacked. We sent up one company to 8th Dubliners left sub section 14 R.I.S. Section) one company to 9 Dubliners in Brigade support as so bombers to be be sublime. Remained as for 25th.	96.
	26/4/16 27/4/16 28/4/16 29/4/16 30/4/16		Moved to "A" Battalion Div. Reserve at MATING A R.S.E. in WHITFORD Rds at Mazingarbe.	96.

Craigh Ashtonal
O.C. 7.I.R. 11SA RIFLES

7 R I Rifles
XVI Vol 6

WAR DIARY
INTELLIGENCE SUMMARY
(Erase heading not required.)

Army Form C. 2118.

Place	Date	Hour	Summary of Events and Information	Remarks and references to Appendices
	1/5/16 to 4/5/16		In billets at PHILOSOPHE EAST as Reserve Battalion of 47th Inf. Bde.	X.
	4/5/16		Relieved 7 LEINSTERS in Right SUB SECTION, HULLUCH SECTION. Attached to 4.9th by Bde.	X.
	4/5/16		Relieved by 9th DUBLINS and moved into Brigade Support. 10th Inf. Casualties 10 O.R. killed, shell fire	X.
	6/5/16		Relieved 9th MUNSTERS in LEFT SUB SECTION – HULLUCH SECTION. 2 O.R. wounded r/f fire	X.
	10/5/16		2nd LIEUT. P.N. HOLDEN wounded (shell fire). 2 O.R. wounded – Grenade.	X.
	11/5/16		Relieved by 9th MUNSTERS and moved into Bde Support. TENTH AVENUE. 3 O.R. wounded A. one O.R. killed A.	X.
	13/5/16		Remained in Bde Support: TENTH AVENUE.	X.
	14/5/16 15/5/16		Relieved 7 LEINSTERS, and 1 Company 6 CONNAUGHTS in RIGHT sub section NEW IU BIS SECTION.	X.
	16/5/16		On 16th 17th 18th 19th. A Coy remained in Bde Support 10th Ave. A Coy remained in Reserve trench.	X.
	20/5/16		On 20th moved to Bde Support 10th Ave. A Coy remained in Reserve trench.	X.
	27/5/16		B Coy relieved A Coy in Reserve Trench.	X.

Army Form C. 2118.

WAR DIARY
INTELLIGENCE SUMMARY.
(Erase heading not required.)

Place	Date	Hour	Summary of Events and Information	Remarks and references to Appendices
	28/5/16		Relieved by 6th CONNAUGHTS. Proceeded to NOEUX LES MINES.	
	29/5/16		Battalion on 2 hour notice for trenches, owing to expected attack by enemy.	
	3/6/16			

Craig Kent Wgh for
A.C.
O.C. 7th (S) Batt ROYAL IRISH RIFLES.

WAR DIARY or INTELLIGENCE SUMMARY

Army Form C. 2118.

June
7th Irish Rifles
Vol 7
XVI

Place	Date	Hour	Summary of Events and Information	Remarks and references to Appendices
NOEUX-LES-MINES	1/6/16	—	In S.W. Reserve at NOEUX-LES-MINES (at halfpay. home leave.)	6.
	2/6/16	—	Relieved 8th BERKS (all 49th Inf Bde) in the LEFT SUB. SECTION, LOOS SECTION. Battalion in NORTH STREET (M.6.B.3,5½) & ENGLISH ALLEY (H 31 a.5½ a.2). 3 Companies in front line, 1 Company in Reserve	70
	3/6/16		Coy fr. 2. Trench mortar and grenade activity on both sides. 3 O.R. killed, 1 wounded.	16.
	4/5/16		Our heavy artillery bombarded SEAFORTH CRATER (N.1.a.0.7) between 5 and 6 p.m.	16.
	5/3/16		We fired rifle grenades into SEAFORTH CRATER as enemy fort line during rifle. 5 O.R. wounded.	16.
	6/5/16		Relieved by 1st MUNSTERS and proceeded to Brigade Reserve PHILOSOPHE EAST. 1 O.R. wounded.	16.
	6/5/16		In Bde Reserve PHILOSOPHE EAST.	16.
	10/5/16		Relieved 1st MUNSTERS in LEFT SUB. SECTION, LOOS SECTION. 3 O.R. killed. 2 O.R. wounded. (A patrol reconnoitred moved N. of SEAFORTH CRATER and found it unoccupied)	16.
	16/5/16		We blew a camouflet at H 31 C.6.2. Crater 20′ x 30′ x 15′ deep use formed. 1 O.R. wounded.	16.
	14/5/16		Heavy rifle grenade fires from both sides. 3 O.R. wounded.	16.
	12/5/16			16

NOEUX-LES-MINES

WAR DIARY
INTELLIGENCE SUMMARY

Army Form C. 2118.

Place	Date	Hour	Summary of Events and Information	Remarks and references to Appendices
	12/6/16		Enemy flare 3 camouflets. 7.50 p.m. at N.1.a.0.8. found a mound 15' high at North side of SEAFORTH CRATER. 10.20 p.m. H.31.C.45.1. Small mound formed.	No
	13/6/16		5.50 a.m. (13) at NEW CRATER (H.31.C.6.2) at entrance party. 3. O.R. wounded. Enemy threw bombs from NEW CRATER (H.31.C.6.2) at entrance party. We retaliated with rifle grenades and Mills grenades, fire from our party.	No.
	14/6/16		Relieved by 3rd Munsters. Went into Bde. Support. H.Q and one Company in VILLAGE LINE G. 28. D.6.5.16 G.34. G.O.2. 1 Coy in DUKE STREET 2 Coys in ENCLOSURE LODS.	No
	15-17			B
	17/6/16		On for 14th Relieved 7th LEINSTERS and forwards killed in MAZINGARBE.	6
	18/4/16		2 Lieuts MOORE, BOYHAN, WILLIAMS joined from 3rd Batt.	No.
	18/6/16		In billets at Mazingarbe.	No.
	20/6/16		Relieved 7th INNISKILLING FUSILIERS and two Companies 8th IRISH FUSILIERS in Brigade support.	No.
	26/6/16		14 Bn SECTION.	
	29/6/16		Raiding party from this battalion arranged to raid enemy trenches opposite H.19.c.9.9 in conjunction with gas, smoke bomb and smoke candles. Operation cancelled at 11 p.m. owing to wind (N.E.)	No.

WAR DIARY
INTELLIGENCE SUMMARY

(Erase heading not required.)

Army Form C. 2118.

Place	Date	Hour	Summary of Events and Information	Remarks and references to Appendices
	27/6/16	11 p.m.	Officers fatal - Capt H.S. ALLISON with M.S. MORTERY - left on trenches at Boyau 67.	A
	28/6/16	1.00 am	See Report "A" attacks. Strong patrol entered sea dept "B" attacks.	B
	29/6/16		In Village line.	X
	30/6/16		Relived 8 Munster in Right Sub Section. 1st Bn section.	X

Brigharstown. To
Lul. OC. 7 Royal Irish Rifle

Report "A"

27/6/16.

Officers Patrol - Capt A.S. ALLISON and
2 Lt. M.J. HARTERY - left BOYAU
67 - H.19. c. 5. 6. - at 11-15 pm,
and crossed to enemy's wire. They found
no gap in the wire but at one place
it was thin. They were seen and
fired at so returned.

The enemy artillery fire on our front line and in front of it was very weak and erratic, but it was heavier on the SUPPORT LINE.

This patrol was commanded by Capt H. S. ALLISON. The other officers on the patrol were
2nd Lt. M. J. HARTERY
2nd Lt. J. KERR.
2nd Lt. J. DEVEREUX.

Report "B"

28/6/16

On the night of the 27th/28th following operations were carried out:-

1 am. 28th Gas was discharged from our front line trenches

1-10 am. Smoke candles were lit on our parapet at intervals of 25yds. Our artillery opened an intense bombardment on enemy's front line.

1-15 am. Gas turned off. "P" Bombs thrown out.

1-20 am. Bombardment changed to slow and continuous.

1-25 am. 2nd "P" bombs thrown out.

1-40 am. Guns lift to enemy's support line.
The advanced party of our strong patrol left our trenches at Boyau 68 with the intention of cutting the wire where patrol "A" had found it thin.

Report "B" (cnt.).

They were followed by the remainder of the raiding party.

The enemy were sending up Very lights along the trench in front and there was some rifle fire.

The advanced party reached the enemy's wire but did not find the thin place. At 1-50 am While at the wire a machine gun opened on them from their left flank.

As they had not got through the wire by 1-55 am — the time arranged for the retirement — they fell back on the covering party and the whole returned to our trench.

Directly in front of where the party went out there was not much activity in the enemy trenches but on either flank flares were sent up continuously and a machine gun was in action.

There was a little rifle fire along the whole line.

At 1-4 am a red rocket was sent up opposite BOYEAU. 67.

Three fires were seen in the enemy's trenches.

July 1916.

W A R   D I A R Y

7th (S) Bn The Royal Irish Rifles

1st. July to 31st. July 1916.

VOLUME No. 8.

WAR DIARY
INTELLIGENCE SUMMARY.
(Erase heading not required.)

Army Form C. 2118.

Place	Date	Hour	Summary of Events and Information	Remarks and references to Appendices
Hd. Zelt	1/7/16	6p	In RIGHT SUB-SECTION, 14 B.S SECTOR. LEFT COMPANY from BOYEAU 55-60. D COY. centre COY BOYEAU 55 - RAILWAY ALLEY C COY.	JA
	2/7/16	6hr	RIGHT COMPANY RAILWAY - ENGLISH ALLEY B COY. A COY IN RESERVE	JA
	3/7/16	6h	On p.m. in MAEATH TRENCH reserves RESERVE TRENCH CHALK PIT on ptn in MAEATH TRENCH - ENGLISH ALLEY. Reports attached.	JA
	3/7/16	10h	Relieved by 1st MUNSTERS and on completion of relief proceeded to PHILOSOPHE being in BRIGADE RESERVE.	JA
	3/7/16 -7/7/16	6p	In BRIGADE RESERVE at PHILOSOPHE	JA
	7/7/16	8pm	Relieved 1st MUNSTERS in RIGHT SUB-SECTION 14 B.S SECTOR taking up same position as on 1/7/16 with exception that B Coy relieved B Coy from RAILWAY ALLEY - ENGLISH ALLEY.	JA
	9/7/16	12h	Patrol of 1 CAPT TLT aco D ART, LIEUT J CRAIG & 2nd LIEUT KERR went to German front lines & placed "gunmen known" made of iron.	JA

WAR DIARY
INTELLIGENCE SUMMARY

Army Form C. 2118.

Place	Date	Hour	Summary of Events and Information	Remarks and references to Appendices
Trenches	10/7/16	6 pm	Lieut J CRAIG wounded.	M
	11/7/16	1 pm	Relieved by 6th ROYAL IRISH REGIMENT and on completion of relief proceeded to Huts at NOEUX-LES-MINES. Lieut J.S. STEELE took over duties of Adjutant vice Lieut & Adjutant J CRAIG wounded.	M
Noeux	11/7/16 – 17/7/16		In Divisional Reserve at NOEUX-LES-MINES.	M
Trenches	18/7/16		Moved into Bde Support in LOOS SECTOR. C & D Coys in ENCLOSURE, LOOS. B Coy in DUKE STREET A Coy & HQrs in VILLAGE LINE.	M
"	20/7/16	3 pm	The Enemy shelled the ENCLOSURE intermittently from the direction of the CITÉ ST AUGUSTE between 8.30 & 10.30 pm.	M
"	21/7/16	3 pm	The Enemy again shelled the ENCLOSURE intermittently. No Casualties. Enemy attitude is very unpredictive, men with field glasses being seen at various points.	M

Army Form C. 2118.

WAR DIARY
or
INTELLIGENCE SUMMARY.
(Erase heading not required.)

Instructions regarding War Diaries and Intelligence Summaries are contained in F. S. Regs., Part II. and the Staff Manual respectively. Title pages will be prepared in manuscript.

Place	Date	Hour	Summary of Events and Information	Remarks and references to Appendices
MAZINGARBE	22/7/16	3 p	The battalion was relieved in Bde support by the 20th Middlesex 40th Division on the night of 22/23 July, proceeded to NORTHERN HUTS MAZINGARBE.	JH
	23/7/16	3 p.m.	Commanding Officer + Coy Comdrs. reconnitred the right sub section HULLUCH	JH
			SECTION	
Trenches	24/7/16	9 p.m.	Bn relieved 7th R. IRISH FUSILIERS 49th Inf Bde in right sub	JH
			section HULLUCH SECTION relief was place as follows.	
			A Coy Right Coy from VENDIN ALLEY inclusive – BOYAU 72 inclus Hav Boy 71	
			B Coy Centre Coy from Boy 72 exclus – Boy 73 inclus, + for German front system 2 Hav Sap-H.z	
			D Coy Left Coy from Boy 73 exclus – Boy 75 exclusive thro SUPPORT LINE	
			C Coy Reserve Coy RESERVE TRENCH, VENDIN exclus to HAY ALLEY inclusive	
			Hars. in 10th A.V. at G.17. d.8.5 H.Qrs 100 yds S.9/HAY ALLEY	JH
Trenches	25/7/16	3 p.m.	Everything very quiet resumed suspers + Rifle grenade fire.	
			Men Flew a Camouflage at 9:50 am near MUNSTER CRATER	
			H 13 a 2.2. Nothing happened the enemy used a search lgt	
			on our front lines. the light appeared to be at PUITS 13 BIS	JH
	26/7/16	3 p.m.	at 5 & 6 pm the enemy shelled our front + support lines, Bombardier from's 1st Austro posn on MUNSTER Crater, he ranging on his batteries all period.	JH

Army Form C. 2118.

WAR DIARY
or
INTELLIGENCE SUMMARY.

(Erase heading not required.)

Place	Date	Hour	Summary of Events and Information	Remarks and references to Appendices
Flanders	27/7/16	5pm	2nd LIEUT P.M. BAILEY 4th LEINSTER REGT joined the day as Signal relieved D Coy in left Coy front. Duty trenches & RESERVE	JS
"	28/7/16	3pm	C Coy. LIEUT KELLY 4 LEINSTER REGT joined LIEUT F.M. MOORE wounded (3)	JS
"	09/7/16	3pm	Comparatively quiet day	JS
"	30/7/16	1pm	1st LIEUTS. CHAWNER, MERRIN & ENGLISH joined	JS
"	31/7/16	8pm	2nd LIEUT KELLY went to hospital suffering from shell shock	JS
"	1/8/16	3pm	Raid on the 31st/1st August was unsuccessful owing to enemy being too soon	JS

J. Steele Lieut & A/Adjt
For Lieut Col
O.C. 7th (S) Bn Royal Irish Rifles
1st August 1916.

Vol 9

WAR DIARY.

7th/ Royal Irish Rifles

MONTH OF AUGUST, 1916.

VOLUME :- 9

WAR DIARY
INTELLIGENCE SUMMARY
(Erase heading not required.)

Army Form C. 2118.

G.4473

7? R. Irish Rifles

Place	Date	Hour	Summary of Events and Information	Remarks and references to Appendices
Vermelles	1/8/16	6.p.m	Relieved 1st RIGHT Subsection HULLUCH SECTION by 1st MUNSTERS and on relief proceeded to BRIGADE RESERVE in VILLAGE LINE at VERMELLES, 2 platoons in OB 1. A Coy } B Coy } 10 ft Ar from WINGS WAY - ESSEY LANE C Coy } OBH fm FOSSE WAY to DEVON LANE D Coy } in CURLEY CRESCENT fm FOSSE WAY - DEVON LANE H.Qrs in FOSSE WAY 20yds WEST of junction of CURLEY CRES & FOSSE WAY. In Brigade Reserve, 2nd Lt MACNAMARA wounded, 2nd Lt FITZMAURICE, PELTON & BOYLE joined.	JH
"	2-4th			JH
"	5/8/16	6pm	Relieved 8th DUBLINS in LEFT SUB-SECTION HULLUCH SECTION Coys temp placed as under, A Coy remaining in OB 1 & Vermelles. B Coy Right Coy. C Coy Centre Coy D Coy Left Coy H.Qrs in OG 1.	JH

WAR DIARY
or
INTELLIGENCE SUMMARY.
(Erase heading not required.)

Army Form C. 2118.

Place	Date	Hour	Summary of Events and Information	Remarks and references to Appendices
Trenches	7/8/16	6pm	Every quiet day except for a run in to dug 7 dump, some damage.	
"	8/8/16	8pm	Relieved by 1st Gloucest Frontline and in relief provided crews HULLOCH SECTION in duty of 1st MUNSTERS & for of 9th DUBLINS. Right of sector Boyau 70. Left of sector Boy 77 Lillicher. C. Coy right Coy from Boy 70 - 73 inclu. A Coy Centre Coy from Boy 73 - 74A inclusive D Coy Left Coy from Boy 74A inclu - Boy 77 inclusive B Coy In Reserve trench from KINGSWAY - ESSEX LANE	
"	9/8/16	3pm	Gas alert, abnormally quiet	
"	10/8/16	3pm	Very quiet days	

Army Form C. 2118.

WAR DIARY
or
INTELLIGENCE SUMMARY.

(Erase heading not required.)

Instructions regarding War Diaries and Intelligence Summaries are contained in F. S. Regs., Part II. and the Staff Manual respectively. Title pages will be prepared in manuscript.

Place	Date	Hour	Summary of Events and Information	Remarks and references to Appendices
Trench	17/8/16	2pm	Relieved by 1st Hunts to a complete of relief foreseen into Brigade Reserve in Billets in Philosophe Street.	JH
Philosophe	12/8/16 –16/8/16		In Brigade Reserve. 2nd Lieut HARVEY & HATTE joined Battn. Cadet School	JH
Trench	16/8/16	3p	Relieved 18th Hunts in left Suffolk Avenue Section on relief by us disposed as follows	
			Arty sppt by Boy 70 – 73	
			B Coy CENTRE Coy Bry 73 – 74a	
			D Coy Left by Bry 74a – 77.	
			C Coy Reserve by ESSEX LANE –	
			WINGS WAY	
Trench	17/8/16	3pm	Quiet day. nothing to report.	
"	18/8/16	3pm	Our artillery carried out a bombardment of the enemy line at 3pm. Good shooting was done, little retaliation.	

WAR DIARY
INTELLIGENCE SUMMARY

Place	Date	Hour	Summary of Events and Information	Remarks and references to Appendices
	19/8/16	5 p.m	Day extremely quiet	
	20/8/16	6 p.m	Relieved in LEFT SEBASTIAN HULLUCH SECTION in conjunction of relief moved into Bde Support in 10th Av. from POSEN ALLEY — WINGS WAY	
20.1.24 8-16			In Bde Support. 1st Lieuts CAPPER & McMULLAN joined 22nd Bn.	
	24/8/16		Relieved in Bde Support by 11th Border Regt 97th Inf Bde in conjunction & proceeded by marched to HOUCHIN where we billeted for the night.	
Allouagne	25/8/16	6 p.m	Marched from HOUCHIN — ALLOUAGNE via BRUAY — MARLES — LOZINGHEM	
"	26/8/16	6 p.m	Brig General Ramsay presented parchment certificates to 31 members of the Battalion.	
Bruay	30/8/16	10 a.m	Bn. Allouagne at 5 a.m on 29th headed to CHELLES where	

Army Form C. 2118.

Army Form C. 2118.

WAR DIARY
or
INTELLIGENCE SUMMARY.
(Erase heading not required.)

Instructions regarding War Diaries and Intelligence Summaries are contained in F. S. Regs., Part II. and the Staff Manual respectively. Title pages will be prepared in manuscript.

Place	Date	Hour	Summary of Events and Information	Remarks and references to Appendices
CORBIE	30/8/16	6 p.	We entrained at 7.12 p.m. Arrived LONGEAU (2 miles EAST of AMIENS) at 4 p.m. marched to CORBIE arriving at 11 a.m.	JA
SAND PIT nr G.I.D N.E. EIII a	31/8/16	8 p.m.	Marched from CORBIE to SAND PIT & took XIVth CORPS RESERVE	JA

J. Steele Lieut Col
for Lieut Col
Cmdg. 1st R.B. Rifle Bde

7/9/16.

Sept 1916

D.A.G. 3rd Echelon Base

Herewith WAR DIARY
for month ending
Sept 30th 1916.

M J Hartery 2/Lt & Adjt
for O.C.
7th R.I. Rifles

1-10-16

WAR DIARY
INTELLIGENCE SUMMARY

7th R.I. Rifles. 48/16

Place	Date	Hour	Summary of Events and Information	Remarks and references to Appendices
SANDPIT Map 62D NE	1/9/16		Remained in SANDPIT for 48 hours. Practised an attack on two lines of trenches, with imaginary creeping barrage of artillery	
Billon Farm	3/9/16	9 AM	Marched from SANDPIT to BILLON FARM arriving at 11.30 A.M.	
CARNOY	3/9/16		Marched from BILLON FARM to CARNOY. Arrived at 6.15 p.m.	
BERNAFAY WOOD	4/9/16	4.0 AM	Left CARNOY and marched to BERNAFAY WOOD into 16th Division	
GUILLEMONT	5/9/16	8 PM	Marched from BERNAFAY WOOD to GUILLEMONT, where we relieved 2 battalions of the 47th Inf. Bde. We remained as garrison of GUILLEMONT – N. until Sept 7th. All this time we were consolidating and digging trenches with the assistance of R.E.s	

WAR DIARY
or
INTELLIGENCE SUMMARY

(Erase heading not required.)

Army Form C. 2118.

Instructions regarding War Diaries and Intelligence Summaries are contained in F.S. Regs., Part II. and the Staff Manual respectively. Title pages will be prepared in manuscript.

Place	Date	Hour	Summary of Events and Information	Remarks and references to Appendices
Guillemont	5/9/16	—	3 strong patrols went out in front of 8th Dublin line to get touch with enemy. They were heavily fired on, and Lieut. H. C. Morgan, and 2/Lieut. A.J. Williams were killed and 2/Lt Munn was wounded.	MJB
"	6/9/16		The following officers were also wounded – 2/Lts Smith, 2/Lt Hannah & 2/Lt Stanowicz on that day. Owing our being garrisoning Guillemont we were very heavily shelled, and suffered many casualties	MJB
				MJB
Trones Wood	7/9/16	6.0 pm	On this evening we relieved the 2 and 6 Border Regts in the front line W1 of GINCHY, where our men spent the night connecting still held to form an Inhabitell system of trenches. A & B Coys were in front line & C & D in support	MJB
			M.O. wounded but still at duty	MJB

Place	Date	Hour	Summary of Events and Information	Remarks and references to Appendices
Front Line W of Ginchy	8/9/16		On the night of the 8th we dug a system of assembly trenches 250 yards in advance of the existing front line with a view to attacking Ginchy on the following day. They were found excellent lines of trenches dug ready the	A.J.F.
	9/9/16		following platoons to make 4 waves of attack. the Bays were placed at Billows. (right to left) R.A.C.D. We were shelled rather heavily and had some casualties. Our stretcher bearers succeeded in bringing in wounded men from our front, who had been lying out since the previous attacks on Ginchy.	A.J.F.
Ginchy	9/9/16 4.45p		On this morning at the hour mentioned our Bn attacked Ginchy. This battalion with the 1st R.M. Fusiliers was the first to enter the village. They succeeded in doing	A.J.F.

WAR DIARY
or
INTELLIGENCE SUMMARY.
(Erase heading not required.)

Army Form C. 2118.

Place	Date	Hour	Summary of Events and Information	Remarks and references to Appendices
Ginchy	9/9/16		and the village was in a good state for defence by	
		12.0 midnight.		
	10/9/16	12.30	At 12.30 AM we were relieved by the WELSH Guards. The enemy made no attempt to counter-attack while we held the village. Our casualties were many wounded Offrs.	
HAPPY VALLEY	10/9/16		After relief we marched back to CARNOY arriving at 7:0 am and leaving at 12.30 in motor lorries for HAPPY VALLEY for our night.	
			We remained in HAPPY VALLEY for our night. The following	
CORBIE	11/9/16	12.14	that we marched to CORBIE arriving at 7:0 p.m.	
"	12/9/16 to		Resting and making up deficiencies in clothing & Sailing	
	19/9/16		a course of Lewis Guns & Bombing. The men to a couple	

WAR DIARY

INTELLIGENCE SUMMARY.

(Erase heading not required.)

Army Form C. 2118.

Place	Date	Hour	Summary of Events and Information	Remarks and references to Appendices
GINCHY	9/9/16	4.45p.	The enemy out of his first line of trench inflicting heavy casualties and taking many prisoners. This was 1st objective but some of the 9th Bn then went on to the second objective with the 9th R. Irish, and had to be forced back after the whole village was in our hands. O.R. killed 39. Wounded, missing &c. 260. The following officers were killed during the attack Major C. Baines, 2/Lt Balfour, 2/Lt Gourley. Wounded – Major Roundtree, Major Lock (died of W.11th) Capt Pogstad, 2/Lt Derrian,	M.J.B. M.J.B.
	9/9/16		Wounded (continued) 2/Lt Boylan (died of W. 12th) 2/Lt Boyle.	M.J.B.
	9/9/16		After capturing the work of consolidation immediately began	

WAR DIARY
INTELLIGENCE SUMMARY.
(Erase heading not required.)

Army Form C. 2118.

Place	Date	Hour	Summary of Events and Information	Remarks and references to Appendices
LONG-PRE	18/9/16	11 A.M.	We left CORBIE at 11 am and proceeded in busses to LONG PRE where we remained until 1.0 A.M on the morning of the 21st	A.J.B
LA CLYTTE	21/9/16	1 P.M.	We entrained at LONG PRE at 1 pm on the 21st and proceeded by rail to GODEWAERSVELDE where we detrained at 10.30 P.M. on the same day. From here we marched to a camp beside LA CLYTTE where we arrived at 5.0 km	A.J.B
	22/9/16			A.J.B
TRENCHES	23/9/16		On the 23rd we left LA CLYTTE to march to the trenches at 4.45 pm. We arrived at Bn. Hqrs at ROSIGNOL at 6.0 p.m. and relieved portion of the 73rd Canadian Battn. in the VAERSTRAAT RIGHT Sub section. Relief was complete at 8.30 P.m. The following was the position of the Coys in the line. Right Front A Coy. Left Front B Coy. Right Support C Coy. Left Support D Coy.	A.J.B
	23/9/16			A.J.B
	24/9/16	3 p.m.	Day extremely quiet. Only a few rum-jars used on our front. These did no damage.	A.J.B

WAR DIARY
or
INTELLIGENCE SUMMARY.

(Erase heading not required.)

Army Form C. 2118.

Place	Date	Hour	Summary of Events and Information	Remarks and references to Appendices
Trucks	25/9/16		Both days were quiet; We had one man killed and one wounded on the 25th by shrapnel.	16/9/16
	27/9/16		Relieved by 12th R ch Fusiliers, and moved into Bde reserve. C + D Coys Bt Hqrs at KLONDYKE FARM. A + B in Bn Reserve in OSSIGNOL WOOD.	17/9/16
	27/9/16			16/9/16
	3/9/16		On Bde Reserve at KLONDYKE FARM.	17/9/16

1-10-16

M.J. Farley 2/Lt a/Adjt
Fr. Lieut-Col
Comdg 7th (S) R.I. Rifles

WAR DIARY

MONTH OF OCTOBER, 1916.

VOLUME 11

7th Royal Irish Rifles.

Army Form C. 2118.

October 1916 WAR DIARY
or
INTELLIGENCE SUMMARY.
(Erase heading not required.)

7th R Irish Rifles

Place	Date	Hour	Summary of Events and Information	Remarks and references to Appendices
Sheet 28.S.W. KLONDYKE FARM Trenches	4/10/16		The Batt. remained in Bde Reserve at KLONDYKE FARM until 5th.	H.S.
	5/10/16		During this time we practised bombing, rifle exercises etc, fitted all ranks with new hose respirator, and supplied fatigues for R.E.	
	6/10/16		We relieved the 1st R.M. Fusiliers in Left Subsection. Relief complete at 5.30 p.m	H.S.
"	7/10/16	6 p.m.	Very quiet day, enemy sent over a few "minnies" but did no damage, and they fell behind the front line. The mortar firing these was suspected at N24.B.3.2. We fired on this point with 18 pdrs silencing the T.M. Another quiet day; a few trench mortars same as yesterday did no damage and were stopped by our artillery. Our Stokes guns scored several direct hits on the enemy's front line	MKB
"	8/10/16	6 p.m	The enemy was a little more aggressive today with trench mortars and rifle grenades but did little damage, and was again stopped by artillery whilst our Stokes fired and gained hits on hostile line at times	HJF
	9/10/16		LIEUTS. T.A. CROUCH; F.S. SIMPSON ; and 2/LIEUT H.M. BOYLE. 3rd R.I.F. vs joined (4th R.I.F.) for duty 2nd	

Army Form C. 2118.

WAR DIARY
or
INTELLIGENCE SUMMARY.
(Erase heading not required.)

Instructions regarding War Diaries and Intelligence Summaries are contained in F.S. Regs., Part II and the Staff Manual respectively. Title pages will be prepared in manuscript.

Place	Date	Hour	Summary of Events and Information	Remarks and references to Appendices
TRENCHES	9/10/16	6pm	Was a quiet day, with the usual few trench mortars, ineffective as before.	
	10/10/16	6am	At about 6am the night boy in the front line asked for retaliation for trench mortars, which we got and stopped the enemy as before. He had only fired a few rounds, and had done no damage. The remainder of the day was quiet.	JJS
	11/10/16		The trench mortar at N.24.B.8.2. was again observed to fire today. Smoke was seen soon after it had fired.	
	12/10/16	3pm	This afternoon the enemy became very aggressive with trench mortars, and aerial torpedoes damaging the front line in four places, and ROSSIGNOL ROAD (communication trench) in three places. Only one of these was badly damaged, and the whole night was spent in repairing it. Two O.R. were wounded, these were the only casualties we had during our tour in the line.	JJS
	13/10/16		2/Lieuts MERRIN and McMULLAN rejoined from Hospital today.	

#353 Wt. W2544/1454 700,000 5/15 D.D.& L. A.D.S.S./Forms/C. 2118.

Army Form C. 2118.

WAR DIARY
or
INTELLIGENCE SUMMARY.
(Erase heading not required.)

Place	Date	Hour	Summary of Events and Information	Remarks and references to Appendices
TRENCHES	12/10/16		LIEUT-COL FRANCIS went on leave. CAPT.H.S.ALLISON took command of the Battalion during his absence.	
	13/10/16		The Bn was relieved by the 1st R.M.Fus and moved into DIVL. RESERVE in LOCRE. As relief in front line was being carried out the enemy again became very aggressive with trench mortars, aerial torpedoes, but did not succeed in getting any into our trenches.	
LOCRE	14/10/16		We were billeted in huts in LOCRE. The first day was spent in cleaning up.	
	15/10/16		Sunday. Church services and baths to-day.	
	16/10/16		The G.O.C. 46th Infy Bde inspected the Bn in the morning. At 12.23 we received a message "TEST GAS ALARM". All ranks were immediately warned and wet box respirators were put on for ten minutes and inspected by officers	

WAR DIARY

Army Form C. 2118.

(Erase heading not required.)

Place	Date	Hour	Summary of Events and Information	Remarks and references to Appendices
LOCRE	17/10/16		Today was spent in training the Coys in Arms drill, Guard mounting, Box respirator Drill, & bombing practice. The L.G. officers started at new classes of newfor boy.	MJJ
	18/10/16		All boys went to the Bombing ground by Bde. H.Q. and everyman threw at least one live bomb.	MJJ
	19/10/16		Training- extended order drill, Physical Drill etc. On 20th new Lewis Gun class fired Lewis Gun. 2/Lieut W.D. LESLIE went to hospital.	MJJ
	20/10/16			
			MAJOR W.T. RIGG joined from 3rd R.I. RIFLES for duty on 19/10/16, and took command of Batt temporarily.	
			Relieved 1st R.M. FUSILIERS in Left But Section, Centre Section. Relief was complete at 5.0 p.m. The boys were disposed as follows	MJJ
TRENCHES	21/10/16		FRONT LINE A" LEFT B Coy, RIGHT Coy C Coy TURNERTOWN RIGHT B" " D " S. P. 12 RESSIGNOL ESTAMINET N.22.a.4.4. (SHEET 28 SW 1/20,000)	MJJ

Army Form C. 2118.

WAR DIARY
or
INTELLIGENCE SUMMARY.
(Erase heading not required.)

Place	Date	Hour	Summary of Events and Information	Remarks and references to Appendices
TRENCHES	22/10/16		Enemy trench mortars were slightly active, but did not damage our line. Our Stokes guns retaliated on enemy front line, and artillery shelled PETIT BOIS causing trench mortars to "shut up". 1 O.R. killed & 1 O.R. wounded.	MHJG
"	23/10/16		Quieter on our front today. 1 O.R. was killed by a bullet on patrol. LIEUT BARNETT went on leave.	
"	24/10/16	1.0 pm	Enemy very active with artillery and trench mortars, but most of those fell on our right. Very few were in our lines. Our heavy artillery retaliated on PETIT BOIS (N2k A+B) with very good effect	MHJG
"	25/10/16	12 noon	and our 18 pounders and Stokes damaged enemy front line. About mid-day the enemy became active again with trench mortars but was very soon silenced by our artillery. LIEUT-Col FRANCIS returned from leave. 2/LIEUT McMULLAN went to hospital	
"	26/10/16		Quiet day. 2/LIEUT McMULLAN went to hospital.	MHJG
	27/10/16		Medium T.M. fired several rounds during the day with good effect. Artillery damaged enemy front line between G & H Sm: entering being part damaged at N94 A6.6 by Lewis gun fire. 2/LIEUT K.E. PAIR went on 8 days leave.	

Army Form C. 2118.

WAR DIARY
or
INTELLIGENCE SUMMARY
(Erase heading not required.)

Place	Date	Hour	Summary of Events and Information	Remarks and references to Appendices
TRENCHES	28/10/16	1:30PM 6:30PM	Our T.M's fired at enemy's wire. Several direct hits were obtained. Enemy T.M's quieter than usual to-day.	
	29/10/16		Relieved by 1/st R.M Fusiliers and moved into B & K RESERVE, with HQ & B.C.D Coy in KEMMEL and A Coy in ROSSIGNOL WOOD	M/Af
	30/10/16		Spent in cleaning new billets and also equipment, clothes etc	
	31/10/16		Baths for half Battalion; remainder training in Box Respirator drill, marching in THREES, and improving billets. Those have not been occupied before & require much cleaning & general improvement.	M/S

for O.C.
M. J. Hartery
Lt 7th R.I. Rifles
1/11/16

WAR DIARY.

FOR

MONTH OF NOVEMBER, 1916.

VOLUME 12

2/7th R. Irish Rifles

Vol 12

Army Form C. 2118.

WAR DIARY
or
INTELLIGENCE SUMMARY
(Erase heading not required.)

1st Woman Rifles

Place	Date	Hour	Summary of Events and Information	Remarks and references to Appendices
SHEET 28 SW 1/20,000 KEMMEL	4/11/16 5/11/16		The Batt. remained in Bde. Reserve training in bombing, guard mounting, squad drill etc. MAJOR RICHMOND, CAPT. KEATING and LIEUT SETH-SMITH joined the batt. for duty on 1.11.16 2/LIEUT GILLIGAN joined on 5.11.16 We relieved the 1st R.M. FUSILIERS in the left sub section to-day. Relief was completed 3.20 p.m. The Coys were disposed as follows Left front line A Coy. Right front line B Coy. TURNERSTOWN RIGHT and FORT MOUNT ROYAL, C Coy. S.P.12 D Coy.	AAA
TRENCHES	6/11/16 7/11/16		The enemy was very quiet to-day. The trenches are in a rather bad state owing to the fallen in in many places owing to the rain. The left Coys lines is particularly bad	AAA

WAR DIARY or INTELLIGENCE SUMMARY

Army Form C. 2118.

Place	Date	Hour	Summary of Events and Information	Remarks and references to Appendices
TRENCHES	8/11/16		Enemy still very quiet. He used neither artillery or trench mortars, nor even in retaliation to our artillery which was fairly active throughout the day.	M/H
	9/11/16	2 p.m	Two enemy shells fell about PARK AVE, but did no damage. These were whizzbangs and came from the direction of WYTCHAETE. Our heavies shelled enemy line in PETIT BOIS between 2 + 3 p.m. with good effect. B b of reserved A Coy in the front line and A Coy relieved D Coy.	
	10/11/16		Our Lewis guns dispersed a working party of hostile N 2 + 8 at about 8.45 p.m. Day quiet.	
	11/11/16			
	22/11/16		At about 2.15 p.m. today enemy bombarded PARK AVE for about half-hour with aerial torpedoes, shrapnel + H.E. No casualties or damage was caused. Our heavies replied and enemy immediately "shoved off". All was quiet at 4.15 p.m.	

WAR DIARY or INTELLIGENCE SUMMARY

Army Form C. 2118.

(Erase heading not required.)

Place	Date	Hour	Summary of Events and Information	Remarks and references to Appendices
TRENCHES	13/11/16		Our trench mortars fired vigorously between 3.20pm & 4.30pm on S. end of PETIT BOIS with very good effect. No retaliation took place.	
	14/11/16		At about 7.45pm the enemy became abnormally active with Trench mortars along our front. We retaliated at 8.15pm with 18 pounders, 4.5" & 6" howitzers, on which outburst the enemy immediately stopped & was quiet during the night. Our firing line was damaged in 3 places. No casualties.	
	15/11/16		Relieved by 1st R.M. Fus and went into Div. RESERVE in LOCRE. B1 Coy was billeted in BIRR BARRACKS.	
	16/11/16		Was spent in general cleaning up & improving drainage. Baths at WESTOUTRE were allotted to & used by the Battalion today.	

WAR DIARY or INTELLIGENCE SUMMARY

Army Form C. 2118.

Place	Date	Hour	Summary of Events and Information	Remarks and references to Appendices
LOCRE	17/11/16		Battalion Route March — LOCRE — WESTOUTRE — RENINGHELST — LA CLYTTE — LOCRE. Working parties supplied for 11th Hants & supplying School MON DES CATS.	
	18/11/16 19/11/16 20/11/16 21/11/16		Remained in Divnl Reserve. 2/LT MAITLAND. W.S. & 108 men joined the Battalion for duty on 21st.	
Sheet 28 SW 20,000 Flanders	22/11/16		Relieved 9th R.D Fusiliers in Right sub-section, Bembroeden 16th Divisional Sector today. Coy disposed as follows D Coy — Right Coy, FRONTLINE B Coy Support Coy C " — LEFT " " " A " RESERVE " Battalion Hd Qrs — DOCTOR'S HOUSE N.21.D.6.6	
"	23/11/16		Enemy very active about 11 p.m. with whizzbangs "Pineapples" & "Rumjars" but was stopped (?) by our artillery. Casualties 1 O.R. Shell Shock. 1 Officer & Medium Trench Mortars were active during the night.	

Army Form C. 2118.

WAR DIARY
or
INTELLIGENCE SUMMARY

(Erase heading not required.)

Place	Date	Hour	Summary of Events and Information	Remarks and references to Appendices
Trenches	23/11/16		Capt David Scollard from Scottish Horse joined for duty tonight.	
"	25/11/16		Lieut Jephale rejoined the Battalion.	
"	28/11/16		Relieved by 9th Dublins. On completion of relief moved into Bde Reserve Section in KEMMEL with Bn HQs at PRIEST'S HOUSE.	
Kemmel	29/11/16		Orders for Lieut Merron to proceed to England to resume his medical studies.	
Kemmel	30/11/16		Lieut Merrin proceeded to England. Lieut Jephale proceeded to England for Cadets 7th R. D. Ref.	

WAR DIARY FOR MONTH OF DECEMBER, 1916.

VOLUME 13

7th R. Irish Rifles

Army Form C. 2118.

WAR DIARY
or
INTELLIGENCE SUMMARY
(Erase heading not required.)

Place	Date	Hour	Summary of Events and Information	Remarks and references to Appendices
Kemmel	1/4/4		Remained in Bde Reserve.	JA
"	6/4		Major W.A. Stirton joined and took over yft extraction. Left extraction & relieved 2nd R. Irish Fusiliers. Left Support in TURNERSTOWN RGT.	GA
			A Coy } Left Support in S.P. 12	
			B Coy } Right Support in Ranph	
			C Coy } In Reserve	
			D Coy } In FRONT LINE.	
London	5.		Slight artillery activity during the afternoon. Shells BROADWAY & behind PH AV.	JA.
"	6/4		At 11 pm a hostile aeroplane was heard E of PETIT Bois, It appeared to come in a southerly direction. OAK TRENCH was Shun in during the morning.	JA

WAR DIARY
or
INTELLIGENCE SUMMARY

(Erase heading not required.)

Army Form C. 2118.

Place	Date	Hour	Summary of Events and Information	Remarks and references to Appendices
Irish tr	7th		Heavy fog + little observation possible. Enemy shelled OAN TRENCH about little damage. Trench mortars + Stokes guns combatted enemy trench during the afternoon.	
"	8th		Still trench mortar activity causing much damage to enemy trenches. Enemy retaliated heavily about 5 p.m. doing little damage. Fog still renders observation difficult.	
"	9th		Quiet all day	
"	10th		Relieved by 9th Duke of & on completion of relief moved into billets in LOCRE having Batt in Bn Reserve at 4 hours notice	
LOCRE	11th		Cleaning up equipment, fitting clothes re. Bathing.	
"	12th		Capt J.D. STEELE took over the duties of Acting Adjt, Major H.S. DE PREE Cpt. P.W. KEATING, the Royal Irish Rifles took over the duties of Attendant	

WAR DIARY or INTELLIGENCE SUMMARY

Army Form C. 2118.

(Erase heading not required.)

Place	Date	Hour	Summary of Events and Information	Remarks and references to Appendices
LOCRE	13/12/16	—	Parades under Cy. arrangements – training in Bombing, Bayonet fighting etc.	AM7
	14/12/16	—	}	
	15/12/16	—	Inspected by the G.O.C. 16th Division, who complimented the men on their smart turn out –	
	16/12/16	—	Relieving 9th Dublins in Regtl. rest. section, 48th Bde. Sector. On relief of Bns. Coys were disposed as follows :—	CMR
			After B Bn — Front Line	
			" C " " S.P.1	
			" D " " TURNERSTOWN RIGHT.	
			" A " " ROSSIGNOL WOOD.	
			H.Q. " " " " OLY ESTAMINET.	
	17/12/16		2nd Lieut V.E. Young rejoined from Transport Lines France. 2nd Lieut O.W. Steeles on reported from Brander Course –	AM7

WAR DIARY
or
INTELLIGENCE SUMMARY

Army Form C. 2118.

(Erase heading not required.)

Instructions regarding War Diaries and Intelligence Summaries are contained in F. S. Regs., Part II. and the Staff Manual respectively. Title Pages will be prepared in manuscript.

Place	Date	Hour	Summary of Events and Information	Remarks and references to Appendices
Dunkirk	17/12		A German was seen about 1 hour opposite SNIPE CORNER. He was moving a few carts out into my huts - had no k. reason given - usual m.g. activity & T.M. activity - Amn b Ltwy frg. visibility poor.	Army
	18/12/16		Very quiet - usual trench Mortar shoots in afternoon.	
	19/12/16		Artillery activity on enemy - Enemy around about 5 or 6 5.9" shells in neighborhood of S.P.12 and TURNERSTOWN.	Army
	20/12/16		Very quiet - situation normal	
	21/12/16		do do 3/R1 N. trench ponies in first-reinforcements	
	22/12/16		Artillery activity shelled TURNERSTOWN - no damage done - moved into B/2e Reserve. Lt J. Kerr struck to Hospital	

Army Form C. 2118.

WAR DIARY
or
INTELLIGENCE SUMMARY

(Erase heading not required.)

Place	Date	Hour	Summary of Events and Information	Remarks and references to Appendices
KEMMEL	25/12		In Bde. Reserve.	Opt
	26/12		All quiet on Christmas Day.	
	27/12		Relieved 9th Battalion in the right subsection, 48th Bde - Reserve - on relief Coys were disposed as follows:-	
			Pokker D Coy - Front line	
			" A " - S.P./12	
			" B " - TURNERSTOWN Rt.	
			" C " - ROSSIGNOL WOOD.	
Trenches	28/12		At 9 am, fire sirens we opened barrage the enemy's front line and wire which had been damaged by our shelling of 26th. No retaliation. Repeated for 2 mins at midnight. Hiss heavily answer when been hostile throwing about unusually mostly that Bde - front on which the bombarded was directed.	

2449 Wt. W14957/M90 750,000 1/16 J.B.C. & A. Forms/C.2118/12.

Army Form C. 2118.

WAR DIARY
or
INTELLIGENCE SUMMARY
(Erase heading not required.)

Place	Date	Hour	Summary of Events and Information	Remarks and references to Appendices
Jenkin	29/1/16		Attack Pelhour 10.30 am & 12.30 pm enemy shelled recruits of LA POLTA - no damage done;	
	30/1/16		Cpl. D. Scotland made a reconnoiss of the lines in front; march N 24.7 returning at N. 24. 6. No wounded enemy mine towards alert; over the trench not occupied.	
	31/1/16		Day quiet - usual T.M. and artillery fire on both sides. 2/Lt. J. Kerr rejoined from Hospital. 2/Lt. M. J. Henderson & 2/Lt. N. Henderson joined from Sch. of Instruction. Lt. H.E. Sith-Smith, 2/Lt. K. Pethan, 2/Lt. N. Brown proceeded to Divisional School 9 am.	

J. Kerr Lieut & A.Adj.

For Lieut Col

C.O. 7th B. Royal Scots Rifles

WAR DIARY for month of JANUARY, 1917.

VOLUME 14

4th Royal Irish Rifles

WAR DIARY
or
INTELLIGENCE SUMMARY

Army Form C. 2118.

Place	Date	Hour	Summary of Events and Information	Remarks and references to Appendices
Near Yares	1/1/17	6 p.m.	Was a very quiet day. Capt Morton (Y.M.) 2nd Lieut Jones W.J. 2nd Lieut Rae (G.S.) 2nd Lieut Wilson W.G. 2nd Lieut Jones.W. joined to-day.	
	2/1/17		Our Trench Mortars supported by Artillery carried out a successful bombardment on enemy front system of trenches, doing much damage to the trenches. The enemy replied with 5.9s in and about S.P.13, it was evident he was trying to knock out our heavy Trench Mortars.	
	3/1/17		Our Vickers Guns fired a good number of rounds, the enemy retaliated with three Rum Jars on LARK LANE doing little damage. Capt Keating left today for Heavy Branch M.G. Corps.	
	4/1/17		Was a very quiet day. A very fine day. A reconnaissance was made by the Battalion Commanding Off. Capt. D. Declare acting Command 2nd Lieut H. Boyle, 2nd Lieut M. Stanley & Capt Barrett	

WAR DIARY
or
INTELLIGENCE SUMMARY

(Erase heading not required.)

Army Form C. 2118.

Place	Date	Hour	Summary of Events and Information	Remarks and references to Appendices
Yprès	4/1/17		The raiding parties (three in all) got into the enemy trench about 3 A.M. and taking the enemy by surprise, inflicted great casualties on them. All our parties returned about 3.45 A.M. having only two men wounded. We "came out" of the line into Bir Reserve LOCRE arriving 2.30 P.M.	
	5/1/17		The Battalion had baths to day.	
	6/1/17		Capt H. Allison, Lieut J. Craig, John J. Hartery, Sgt E. Bailey and Sgt T. Hosey were mentioned in Sir Douglas Haig's despatches.	

Army Form C. 2118.

WAR DIARY
or
INTELLIGENCE SUMMARY
(Erase heading not required.)

Instructions regarding War Diaries and Intelligence Summaries are contained in F. S. Regs., Part II and the Staff Manual respectively. Title Pages will be prepared in manuscript.

Place	Date	Hour	Summary of Events and Information	Remarks and references to Appendices
	7/1/17		The Companies paraded today under Company arrangements. Lieut Y. a. Crowe left today for the Heavy Branch M.G.C.	
	8/1/17		Battalion had a Route March today. Major Rigg took over command. The Commanding Officer went on leave.	
	9/1/17		D Company were Bombing & in the open bombing ground from 9.30 am to 12 noon. C. Company from 2 P.m. to 4 P.m. 2nd Lieut J Barry and 2nd Lieut G Maguire 4th Connaught Rangers joined today.	

2449 Wt. W14957/M90 750,000 1/16 J.B.C. & A. Forms/C.2118/12.

WAR DIARY or INTELLIGENCE SUMMARY

Army Form C. 2118.

Place	Date	Hour	Summary of Events and Information	Remarks and references to Appendices
Street 20/SW 20000	10/7/17		2/Lieut H.V. Moore & 2/Lieut A.E. Butler 4th Connaught Rangers joined to day for duty. D Company were bombing at the Bog. bombing ground from 9-30 A.m. to 12 noon. C Company from 2 P.m. to 4 P.m.	
	11/7/17		Companies training under Company arrangements	
Yvrench	12/7/17		The Battalion relieved the 9th R. Dublin Fus. in the line (Right Bat. sector) Relief completed by 4.0 P.m. A Company - Front line C " - Turner Right. D " - Banff Dugouts. 1 Platoon in Parr Ave. B " - Rossignol. 1 Platoon in Fort Royal.	

Army Form C. 2118.

WAR DIARY
or
INTELLIGENCE SUMMARY

(Erase heading not required.)

Instructions regarding War Diaries and Intelligence Summaries are contained in F. S. Regs., Part II and the Staff Manual respectively. Title Pages will be prepared in manuscript.

Place	Date	Hour	Summary of Events and Information	Remarks and references to Appendices
Yrseles	13/7/17		The day was very quiet, except for a little activity with T.M's on both sides between 2-3.30 P.m. Relieved A.C.O. Hill from the 4th R.S. Rifles. James no today for duty.	
	14/7/17		At 9.30 P.m. in reply to our artillery activity, the enemy fired T.M's aerial torpedoes and rifle grenades on our front line PARIT AVENUE. BANFF DUGOUTS. doing no damage. Our Stokes gune replied to and silenced hostile T.M's firing 80 rounds	
	15/7/17		The day passed very quietly	
	16/7/17		Our T.M's bombarded enemy front line. Good shooting was made. Some 4.2's were fired on PARIT AVENUE + BANFF DUGOUTS. No damage was done	

WAR DIARY
or
INTELLIGENCE SUMMARY

Army Form C. 2118.

Place	Date	Hour	Summary of Events and Information	Remarks and references to Appendices
Yraneles	17/1/17		Was a very quiet day with the usual few trench mortars ineffective as before. One of our Lewis Guns effectively engaged a party of the enemy which were working on their wire.	
	18/1/17		Nothing of importance happened today	
	19/1/17		All quiet today	
	20/1/17		The 9th R. Irish Fus. relieved us today. we moved back to Bgde Reserve with 3 Coys at BUTTERFLY FARM & one Coy in KEMMEL. Coy in KEMMEL was detailed to hold VIERSTRAAT SWITCH	

Place	Date	Hour	Summary of Events and Information	Remarks and references to Appendices
	20-1-17		The following Officers joined the Bn & were posted to Coys as follows:- Lieut Oakshott (Munster) A Coy, Lieut Wyvill (A Coy), Lieut Byrne (Munster) D Coy, 2nd Lt Roche (Munster) B Coy, 2nd Lieut St. Pope (Connaught) C Coy, 2nd Lieut Lane (on first attachment) C Coy, 2nd Lieut Dwight (from 14 Bn R. Ir. Rif. B Coy, Major Richmond & 2nd Lieut Butler proceeded on	
	21-1-17		Major Richmond & 2nd Lieut Butler proceeded on leave.	JS
	24-1-17		Aeroplane Contact Achievements Brigade arrangements	
	29-1-17		Relieved 9th R Dub Fus in the right subsection Vinestreet Section, C Coy in front line, B & A Coys in support in BANFF DUGOUTS, TURNERSTOWN RIGHT & T respecting D Coy in Reserve at ROSSIGNOL CAP JS St[...] Relieved from 48 Inf. Bde.	JS

WAR DIARY
or
INTELLIGENCE SUMMARY

Army Form C. 2118.

Place	Date	Hour	Summary of Events and Information	Remarks and references to Appendices
Lindic	29/1/17		The Bn front was reorganised. Intended Southward taking in BROADWAY. B Coy relieved 7/8 Inat Fusiliers from BROADWAY - ASH LANE. D Coy relieved B Coy in BANFF. 2nd Lieuts Kenny on platoon Resigno L Ennis, Moore & Maguire returned from leave & joined their own platoons. 2nd Lieut Smith relieved 2nd Lieut Cawston one O.R. wounded at duty. (Lieut Huffam M.O. is ready)	fd
"	30/1/17			fd
"	31/1/17		Lt. Col. Farmer D.S.O. relieved from leave & resumed command of Bn. Battalion strength 2nd Lieut V.M. Moore went to 48 T.M.B.	fd

1-2-17.

J. A. Meek Captain & A/Adjt.
for Lieut Col Cmdg
7th R. I. Rifles

WAR DIARY.

FOR MONTH OF FEBRUARY, 1917.

VOLUME 15

UNIT:- 7th Royal Irish Rifles

Vol 15

Army Form C. 2118.

WAR DIARY
INTELLIGENCE SUMMARY

February 1917

(Erase heading not required.)

Instructions regarding War Diaries and Intelligence
Summaries are contained in F. S. Regs., Part II
and the Staff Manual respectively. Title Pages
will be prepared in manuscript.

Place	Date	Hour	Summary of Events and Information	Remarks and references to Appendices
Franklin	1-2-17		2nd Lieut K K Butler transferred (temply) A Coy to left Coy. 2nd Lieut B Coy in centre Coy (repl) C Coy relieved C Coy in left Coy. front line; Coln Butalion & Bgm McColm remainder for Wiebels Woeten & Chalet front line respectively. Quiet day.	JH
"	2-2-17			JH
"	3-2-17		Major Richmond & Lieut Butler returned from leave. Capt Geo Ramsey proceeded Parachute Catechules to 4 Affleurs & 12 men for musl due on 4th January 1917.	JH
"	4-2-17		Lieut W Francis DSO went to Brig HQrs. Gen Ramsey going on 3 weeks leave Major Ryft assumed Command.	JH
"	5-2-17		Relieved by 9th Batthns and on completing relief moved into Bde Reserve at BIRR BARRACKS LOCRE at 2 hours notice.	JH
Locre	6-2-17		2nd Lieut BEATTY, 2nd LIEUT THOMPSON, 2nd Lieut HOOPS & 2nd Lieut CORRIGAN & all C & R Draft trawlmen joined for duty.	JH
"	7-2-17		The Battalion for a Change of underclothing as WESTOUTRE first being still known no waters was available C.O. had Conference of Coy Commanders.	JH

Army Form C. 2118.

WAR DIARY
or
INTELLIGENCE SUMMARY

(Erase heading not required.)

Instructions regarding War Diaries and Intelligence Summaries are contained in F. S. Regs., Part II and the Staff Manual respectively. Title Pages will be prepared in manuscript.

Place	Date	Hour	Summary of Events and Information	Remarks and references to Appendices
LOCRE	8/2/17		Draft B 14 men arrived. All old men & reported to former companies.	JH.
"	9.2.17		Battalion Route March. Route LOCRE — MONTDIR via BAILLEUL ROAD WESTOUTRE — LOCRE. James in the afternoon.	JH.
"	11-2-17		2nd LIEUT POE went to hospital. LIEUT B.G.SHAVE joined 48" T.M.B. at KEMMEL	JH.
"	12-2-17		C.O. & O.C. D + A C nº reconnoitred line to be taken over on 13th inst. Baths during the afternoon.	JH.
Trenches	13-2-17		Relieved 9th Dublins in Right Sub sector VIERSTRAAT SECTION. the following were the dispositions. A Coy Right Cy D Coy Right Cy C Cy S.R. 12 with 1 platoon at ROSSIGNOL B Coy Reserve Right Lieut Willis Brevet Grenade Course. Lewis Hopk provided on Platfr Gun Couple	JH.

Army Form C. 2118.

WAR DIARY
or
INTELLIGENCE SUMMARY.
(Erase heading not required.)

Instructions regarding War Diaries and Intelligence Summaries are contained in F. S. Regs., Part II. and the Staff Manual respectively. Title pages will be prepared in manuscript.

Place	Date	Hour	Summary of Events and Information	Remarks and references to Appendices
Trenches	14-2-17		Several hostile aeroplanes flew over our lines during the day. Enemy M.G. was active in S.P.12 during the night. Casualties nil	ff
	15-2-17		At 9 am several 77 mm shells were fired in on our front line from N24.4. – N24.B.8 trench is being used at N24.a.8.9.	ff
Trenches	16-2-17		Our artillery was very active. Enemy artillery not to active as usual. A working party was dispersed by our Lewis Guns opposite N24.4. Enemy wounded on V.C. road by M.G. fire. Casualties. 2 O.R. wounded. Lieut. Berry & Hackett patrols Returned	ff
	17-2-17		Enemy heavy artillery fire on our batteries. Casualties were very few	ff
	18-2-17		Our artillery bombarded Enemy T.M. emplacements with good effect. At 9 pm there was heavy M.G. fire on OAK TRENCH.	ff
	19-2-17		Quiet. O.M. at LOCRE. LIEUT V. ZIELLI & LIEUT HOPPS returned from Courses 2nd Lieut. CORRIGAN provided on Stokes Course.	M

WAR DIARY
or
INTELLIGENCE SUMMARY.
(Erase heading not required.)

Army Form C. 2118.

Place	Date	Hour	Summary of Events and Information	Remarks and references to Appendices
Trenches	20-2-17		Heavy artillery fire on PARK AV, OAK TRENCH & ASH LANE, about 200 S.9.0 were fired in reply from Corps Heavies. 2 Officers Casualties were Blown in & Right Coy Signal Officer was hit. Casualties 1 OR wounded (at duty.)	Yes
"	21-2-17		Relieved by 9th DUBLINS on completion of relief moved to BUTTERFLY FARM & became Battalion in Bde Support at 2 hours notice. 1 NCO + 12 men lave for Railway Construction.	"
BUTTERFLY FARM	22-2-17		In BUTTERFLY FARM. Battalion had baths at LOCRE 9½ - 12 am	"
"	23-2-17		Lewis Gun Course, Sniping Course, & Bayonet fighting course commenced.	Yes
"	25-2-17		2nd Lieuts J. Ellyan & Beatty proceeded to Div Sch M on Vong Officer Course, 2nd Lieut Hill returned. 2nd Lieut Dwyer R.F.A. as instructor.	Yes

Army Form C. 2118.

WAR DIARY
or
INTELLIGENCE SUMMARY.
(Erase heading not required.)

Place	Date	Hour	Summary of Events and Information	Remarks and references to Appendices
Butterfly Farm	26-2-17		Lieut L.H. Taylor Transport Officer proceeded to England. 2nd Lieut W.S Maitland we took over the Transport.	JR
Butterfly Farm	27-2-17		Major A.H. R. Richmond proceeded to 3rd Army H/Qrs as "Learner" Lieut A.J Francis D.S.O returned from Bde.	JR
Butterfly Farm	28-2-17		Firing on Musketry Range. A Coy on Bombing Ground during the morning.	M

28-2-17.

J.R.H. Searle Capt & A/Adjt
for Lieut Col R
Cmdg 7th R.J Rifles

WAR DIARY
FOR MONTH OF MARCH, 1917.

VOLUME 16

UNIT:- 7th Royal Irish Rifles

Army Form C. 2118.

WAR DIARY
or
INTELLIGENCE SUMMARY.
(Erase heading not required.)

Place	Date	Hour	Summary of Events and Information	Remarks and references to Appendices
Trenches	1-3-17		Relieved 9th R. Irish Rif. in the Right Sub-section Left Section. B Coy. Right Coy. C Coy Left Coy. D Coy in Support at TURNERSTOWN + A Coy in Reserve at BAMFF DUGOUTS. HQ at FORT MOUNT ROYAL + 1 pltn in ROSSIGNOL. HQ in ROSSIGNOL ROAD.	
"	2-3-17		Very quiet day + exceptionally quiet night	
"	3-3-17		Enemy were suddenly repeatedly along the line BYRON FARM – WATLING ST. – VAN KEEP – SP 12. Quiet at night	
"	4-3-17		Considerable artillery activity on both sides. A Right front. D Left front. C Turnerstown + B Bamff dugouts. Capt. Rev O'Reilly at BUTTERFLY FARM	
"	5-3-17		Draft of 14 men arrived. nearly all from Leinster Reg.	
"	6-3-17		Our artillery was very active all day + all night	

WAR DIARY or INTELLIGENCE SUMMARY

Army Form C. 2118.

Place	Date	Hour	Summary of Events and Information	Remarks and references to Appendices
Trenches	7-3-17		Enemy T.M. at N.24.C.9.4. was active & Cavalry both artillery BROADWAY, PARK AV & S.P. 12 were shelled with 4.2's & 5.9's but was located at N.18 & I.S.	
"	8-3-17 11am		From 10 am – 2.35 pm there was intermittent both shell fire and T.M. fire on our front & support lines. At 3:30 pm the enemy commenced a heavy T.M. + artillery bombardment on the Battalion front. At 4:40 pm under cover of an intense barrage enemy attacked in three parties approximately 50 men each. The right party were beaten by our Lewis gun fire & centre & left attacking parties entered our trenches at N2 4.7 & N2 6.9. some of these parties penetrated to PARK AV They were driven back by counter attack within 15 minutes leaving 3 dead + 4 wounded in our hands.	

WAR DIARY
or
INTELLIGENCE SUMMARY

Army Form C. 2118.

Place	Date	Hour	Summary of Events and Information	Remarks and references to Appendices
	8-3-17	Continued	Major Ruff led the Counter attack with great gallantry & Lieut Potts. Casualties amongst the Army N.C.O. Lieut. Huxley was Killed. Capt. Bennett wounded, Lieuts Thompson, Bergin & Owens wounded & 2nd Lieut. Young & Morton wounded but remained at duty. Other ranks 7 O.R. Killed 31 wounded & 25 missing.	JS
	9-3-17		Relieved by 9th R. Irish. Fus. Withdrew to BIRR BARRACKS. LOCRE known as in Bde reserve at 2 hours notice.	JS
	10-3-17		Battalion had baths at WESTOUTRE.	JS
	11-3-17		Training commenced. Squadly Class & Lewis gun classes formed.	JS
	12-3-17		Nothing to report.	JS
	13-3-17		Nothing to report.	JS
	14-3-17		Training happening as usual.	JS

WAR DIARY
or
INTELLIGENCE SUMMARY.

Army Form C. 2118.

Place	Date	Hour	Summary of Events and Information	Remarks and references to Appendices
LOCRE	15-3-17		Bn. Route March. Gen. Hickie inspected the billets.	JH
LOCRE	16-19-3-17		Coy training being carried out	JH
"	19-3-17		Reconstruction of Div. Front. One Bn in front, one in support + one in reserve. Draft of 83 men rcd. Bn. moved from BIRR BARRACKS to CURRAGH CAMP and there were billeted with 9th R.D.V.B. Two they having all the W. Res. We hilt an orderly room immediately. Draft of 26 men rcd.	JH
"	20-3-17		Draft of 10 men received.	JH
"	20-21-3-17		Coy Training under new O.T.B. 1917 scheme. 2nd Lieuts Green + Wolffe joined on 25-3-17. Lieut Helan rejoined from Hospital on same date. 2nd Lt Gillespie transferred to G. RANTAAM to M.G. Corps. Major Ryff went to divine 21st inst. Capt SCOTT went on 20th inst.	JH

A 534. Wt. W4973/M687. 750,000. 8/16. D. D. & L. Ltd. Forms/C.2118/13.

Army Form C. 2118.

WAR DIARY
or
INTELLIGENCE SUMMARY.
(Erase heading not required.)

Instructions regarding War Diaries and Intelligence Summaries are contained in F.S. Regs., Part II. and the Staff Manual respectively. Title pages will be prepared in manuscript.

Place	Date	Hour	Summary of Events and Information	Remarks and references to Appendices
LOCRE	28-3-17		154 men on working parties under R.E.	
LOCRE	29+30-3-17		Still in CURRAGH CAMP preparing to march to 2nd Army Training Area	
HAZEBROUCK	31-3-17		Bn marched from LOCRE to HAZEBROUCK via BAILLEUL. Left LOCRE 9 am. Arrived HAZEBROUCK 3.30 pm. Snowing on the way. Fair weather. The snow fell not in March	

2/4/17.

J. Alfred Cullimore
Lt. Col.
OC 7th R. Ir. Rifles

WAR DIARY FOR MONTH OF APRIL, 1917.

VOLUME:- 17

UNIT:- 7th R. Irish Rifles

Army Form C. 2118.

7/Royal Irish Rifles.

April 1917

WAR DIARY
or
INTELLIGENCE SUMMARY.
(Erase heading not required.)

Instructions regarding War Diaries and Intelligence Summaries are contained in F.S. Regs., Part II. and the Staff Manual respectively. Title pages will be prepared in manuscript.

Place	Date	Hour	Summary of Events and Information	Remarks and references to Appendices
HALLINES	1-4-17		Battalion marched to HALLINES being at 9 a.m. and marching via ARQUES arriving HALLINES 4 p.m. Very from WEEK. 3 men fell out on march.	M
TOURNEHEM	2-4-17		Battalion marched to TOURNEHEM from HALLINES via SEQUES – QUELQUES – QUE RAMP – arriving at 2.45 p.m. arriving in the way. No men fell out. C/N. Scotland returned from leave 2nd Lt Greene reported from Grenade course	M
TOURNEHEM	3-4-17		the Battalion had baths. Companies commenced Coy training	M
"	4-4-17		Coy training continued Major W.J. Ryff returned from leave	M
"	5-4-17		Coy training continued (Trench to trench attack)	M
"	6-4-17		Final day B Coy training (Tactical Schemes)	M

Army Form C. 2118.

WAR DIARY
INTELLIGENCE SUMMARY.
(Erase heading not required.)

Place	Date	Hour	Summary of Events and Information	Remarks and references to Appendices
TOURNEHEM	7-4-17		Battalion training Commenced. Battalion advancing in artillery formation changed to attack formation. Battalion advances from position to rendering S.W. of NORTKERLINGHEM preceded by Scouts in artillery formation chap to attack formation on enemy under fire from enemy on road S.E. of LA RONVILLE. Draft of 77 men arrived.	
"	8-4-17		Battalion training. Battalion in attack passing from one objective to another.	
"	9-4-17		Battalion training. Battalion in pursuit passing through wooded country & approaching a village. 2nd Lieut. HARPER, BUTZER & HOPS proceeded to HAZEBROUCK for interview for Royal Flying Corps	
"	10-4-17		Outpost Scheme in Final day of Battalion training. Musketry Competition Platoons of 32 rifles, 2 minutes - rapid fire. No 1 Platoon D Coy won Battalion Competition.	
"	11-4-17		Brigade Training Commences. Battalion to practice attack exercise the Carried out at 12th Welch V	

Army Form C. 2118.

WAR DIARY
or
INTELLIGENCE SUMMARY.
(Erase heading not required.)

HAZEBROUCK &c. 1a 108, OB.

Place	Date	Hour	Summary of Events and Information	Remarks and references to Appendices
TOURNEHEM	12/4/17		Attack Exercise carried out as Brigade training. The Battalion was in front line in Right supported by 9th R. Bde. Inv. Final of Bde Competition. Company training.	Yes
"	13/4/17			Yes
"	14-4-17		Bde Training Final day. Practice attack Parade 8am. Back in billets at 1pm. Capt R.L. Henderson a+R.I. Reg. reported for duty.	Yes
LOCRE	15-4-17		Battalion marched from TOURNEHEM. B.C.+D Coys complete with 50 men from A Coy + 20 from Bn Hqrs. proceeded by lorry to LOCRE together with cookers. Rear staff. A Coy and remainder of Bn Hqrs with T. transport marched to Billets in HALLINES. Major Rifft proceeded on 3 days leave in England whilst Bn was at BAILLEUL.	Yes
"	16-4-17		Working Parties to C.R.E. provided by B.C.+D Coys. A Coy + Bn Hqrs marched from HALLINES to HAZEBROUCK. No men fell out.	Yes
"	17-4-17		Working Parties by B.C.+D Coys. A Coy+Hqrs marched from HAZEBROUCK to LOCRE. BIRR BARRACKS. Marched past Lt General Godley Cmdg ANZAC Corps in BAILLEUL	Yes

WAR DIARY
or
INTELLIGENCE SUMMARY.

Army Form C. 2118.

Place	Date	Hour	Summary of Events and Information	Remarks and references to Appendices
LOC RE	18-4-17		Working Parties for CRE while GOC practically the whole Battalion. C.O. & OC Coys made a reconnaissance of VIERSTRAAT SECTOR.	JH
Trenches	19-4-17		Bn. relieved 6th Connaught Rangers in Rykenhock VIERSTRAAT SECTOR. Coys were disposed as follows.	JH
			B Coy. Right front Coy from KETCHEN AV to ASH LANE	
			D Coy. Left " " from ASH LANE to LARK LANE	
			A Coy. Right support Coy in SP11 & ALBERTA DUGOUTS	
			C Coy. Left " " in SP12 & BANFF DUGOUTS	
			Bn. HQrs in TURNERSTOWN & CHINESE WALL.	JH
			Lieut OAKSHOTT went to hospital	
"	20-4-17		Very quiet day. Our artillery was pretty active but enemy did not reply.	JH
"	21-4-17		Quiet. Patrol consisting of Capt SCOTTARD NC & 4 other Ranks left our own trench at No 4.8 at 2:30 am when about to get into German trench they were attacked. Capt SCOTTARD & 2 other Ranks are missing. the other two returned both severely wounded	JH

Army Form C. 2118.

WAR DIARY
or
INTELLIGENCE SUMMARY.
(Erase heading not required.)

Place	Date	Hour	Summary of Events and Information	Remarks and references to Appendices
Trenches	22-4-17		Battalion to report. 2nd Lieuts Mcguire & Lane returned from 16th Div. School.	
"	23-4-17		A Coy relieved B Coy in Right Front line. B Coy moved into Right support. C Coy relieved D Coy in Left front line. D Coy moved into left support. 2nd Lieut Ref Hunter proceeded to 2nd army Hypnally School on Course, 2nd Lieut Aitchell took over the duties of Hypnally Officer.	
"	24-4-17		Very Quiet. Nothing to report.	
"	25-4-17		Much artillery activity on both sides during the night.	
"	26-4-17	9.45 T.M.	fired between the lines 9 & 5 pm. Much damage was done to German trenches.	
ROSSIGNOL ESTAMINET.	27-4-17		Bn was relieved by 9th R. Irish Fus. & on relief became Bn in Bde support with Headquarters at ROSSIGNOL ESTAMINET. A Coy wih HELLELEUM, LA POLKA & DOCTOR'S HOUSE. B Coy in ROSSIGNOL FARM. C Coy in SIEGE TRENCH. D Coy in SIEGE FARM with 1 Platoon in SAND BAG VILLA.	

Army Form C. 2118.

WAR DIARY
or
INTELLIGENCE SUMMARY.
(Erase heading not required.)

Place	Date	Hour	Summary of Events and Information	Remarks and references to Appendices
ROCSIGNOL ESTAMINET	28-4-17		Nothing to report. Bde Support supplying working Parties. Casualties 1 o.r. Killed, 1 wounded.	AA.
"	29-4-17		Quiet. LIEUT T. KERR proceeded on leave.	AA.
"	30-4-17		LIEUT & ADJT T. Craig joined & also Lieut G. B. J. Smith 5th Bn R.I. Rifles. 1 man killed & 6 wounded. Strength at opening of month 33 Officers + 693 other Ranks Strength at end of month 32 Officers + 829 other Ranks.	AA.

36-4-17.

J. Steele Capt. & A/Adjt
for O.C. 7th R.I. Rifles.

W A R   D I A R Y :

VOLUME:- 18

FOR MONTH OF MAY, 1917.

UNIT:- 7th R. Irish Rifles

WAR DIARY
or
INTELLIGENCE SUMMARY.

(Erase heading not required.)

Army Form C. 2118.

Place	Date	Hour	Summary of Events and Information	Remarks and references to Appendices
ROSSIGNOL ESTAMINET	1/5/17		2nd Bn Support. Lieut Col Francis DSO proceeded on leave, Major Ryst assumed Command of the Battalion.	H
"	2/5/17		Nothing to report.	H
"	3rd & 4/5/17		Working parties as usual.	H
DE ZON CAMP.	5/5/17		Battalion was relieved in Bde Support by the 7th Leinster Regt and on completion of relief moved to DE ZON CAMP (N12 c L5).	H
"	6/5/17		2nd Lieut LANE proceeded on leave. Battalion had baths at WESTOUTRE	H
"	7/5/17		Company training in formations to attack lines.	H
"	8/5/17		16 NCOs & 8 Officers attended wiring demonstration given by Major Whorff 157th Field Coy R.E. Very good.	H

WAR DIARY
or
INTELLIGENCE SUMMARY

Army Form C. 2118.

Place	Date	Hour	Summary of Events and Information	Remarks and references to Appendices
~~BUSSEBOOM~~ KEMMEL SHELTERS	9/5/17.		Company training as usual after having Marched to KEMMEL SHELTERS. 3 Ptes A Coy were billeted in DONCASTER HUTS.	JH
KEMMEL	10/5/17.		LOCRE. The remainder of Battalion at KEMMEL SHELTERS. Capt R.L. Henderson went to Hospital.	JH
"			A + B Coys proceeded to RENINGHELST joined Battalion 2nd Lts IRWIN and CRAWFORD joined Battalion	JH
BIRR BARRACKS	11/5/17		C + D Coys and Battalion HQrs moved from KEMMEL SHELTERS, Day and HQrs to BIRR BARRACKS; C Coy to DONCASTER HUTS.	JH
"	12/5/17.		WORKING PARTIES.	JH
"	13/5/17		Col Francis DSO. returned from leave and also Lieut J. Kerr A+B Coys returned to DONCASTER HUTS.	JH
"	14/5/17		Draft of 99 men arrived.	JH

Army Form C. 2118.

WAR DIARY

(Erase heading not required.)

Place	Date	Hour	Summary of Events and Information	Remarks and references to Appendices
BIRR BARRACKS	15-5-17 to 18-5-17		Working Parties, CAPT. McMASTER M.C. reported for duty 17th inst, 2nd Lieut A. Brown rejoined. Major Allim rested on leave 16-5-17 2nd Lyall 15/5/17	AA.
Trenches	18-5-17.		Lieut A.N. OAKSHOT returned from Hospital Lieut Wilson went on leave 18-5-17 Battalion relieved 7/8th R. IR. FUS. in left sub-section VIERSTRAAT SECTOR taking up the following dispositions. C & D Coys in Front line (C Coy on Right) B Coy in SP 13 and VAN KEEP. A Coy in CHINESE WALL LINE. Bn HQrs at YORK HOUSE	AA. AA.
"	19/5/17.		Quiet except for not artillery which fires all the time	AA.
"	20/5/17		2nd Lieuts E.S. HATTE and HANNAH rejoined Battalion. Draft of 12 men received	AA.

Army Form C. 2118.

WAR DIARY
or
INTELLIGENCE SUMMARY.
(Erase heading not required.)

Place	Date	Hour	Summary of Events and Information	Remarks and references to Appendices
Trenches	21-5-17		Our Artillery showed considerable activity. GRAND BOIS and UNNAMED WOOD was heavily shelled.	JH
"	22-5-17		Very quiet day.	
"	23-5-17		The Battalion carried out a small surprise raid against the enemy trenches at N.18.b - 20.30. Three Officers & 44 Other Ranks was the strength of the raiding party. Lieut J.C.May was in charge. The other two Officers were 2nd Lieut R.V.Bright and 2nd Lieut A.D.Hill (separate report attached)	JH 2 officers 1
"	24-5-17		Our artillery was very active. Little enemy retaliation	JH
"	25-5-17		Enemy shelled S.P.13 intermittently during the day - otherwise very quiet	JH

Army Form C. 2118.

WAR DIARY
or
INTELLIGENCE SUMMARY.
(Erase heading not required.)

Army Form W. 20,000

Place	Date	Hour	Summary of Events and Information	Remarks and references to Appendices
BUTTERFLY FARM	26-5-17		Battalion was relieved by the 9th R. Dub. Fus. and on completion of relief moved to BUTTERFLY FARM forming Battalion in Bde Reserve. The following Officers returned in from Brigade H.Qrs. Details: Capt J. Steele, Lieut W. Knipton, Lieut J. Kerr, C.S.M. D. Authorau.	AA
"	27/5/17		Cleaning up and Church Parades. Big raid Carried out by 2nd R. Dub. Fus. resulting in 1 Officer & 30 German being taken prisoner. Our Casualties were light.	AA
"	28/5/17		Enemy shelled Camps intermittently during the night. 2 men were wounded & 1 shell shock	AA
"	29/5/17		Nothing to report	AA

Army Form C. 2118.

WAR DIARY
or
INTELLIGENCE SUMMARY.
(Erase heading not required.)

Place	Date	Hour	Summary of Events and Information	Remarks and references to Appendices
BUTTERFLY FARM	30-5-17		Major H.S. Allison returned from leave; 2nd Lieut Hartley returned from Artillery School.	JA
"	31-5-17		C.S.M. D'AUTHREAU awarded Medaile Militaire by President French Republic. 2nd Lieut A. Brown proceed to T.M. Battery. Strength on 1st May 1917. 32 Officers + 829 Other Ranks Strength on 31st May 1917 40 Officers + 940 Other Ranks	JA JA
				J. Allen Capt + Adjt for Lieut Col CO 7th R.I. Rifles
			31/5/17	

WAR DIARY.

FOR MONTH OF JUNE, 1917.

VOLUME:- 19

UNIT:- 7b (S) Battn Royal Irish Rifles

Army Form C. 2118.

WAR DIARY
or
INTELLIGENCE SUMMARY.
(Erase heading not required.)

June 1917

R/ 5 W 20 AD

Place	Date	Hour	Summary of Events and Information	Remarks and references to Appendices
BUTTERFLY FARM	1/6/17		Company training carried on as usual	
CLARE CAMP	2/6/17		Battalion was relieved in BUTTERFLY FARM by 7" R. INNIS. Fus & on completion of relief moved to CLARE CAMP being Battalion in Bde. Reserve.	
"	3/6/17		Conference of CO's at Bde Office. Church Parade.	
"	4/6/17		Training under Company arrangements. Enemy fired a few shells into Camp at about 6 p.m. Bttn had no casualties but 2 officers of 2nd R. Dub. Fus were killed.	
"	5/6/17		Company training as usual.	

WAR DIARY
or
INTELLIGENCE SUMMARY.
(Erase heading not required.)

Army Form C. 2118.

Place	Date	Hour	Summary of Events and Information	Remarks and references to Appendices
Staine Camp	6/6/17		Bttn parade 10 a.m. Inspection by C.O. of units etc. Temp shelled during the morning, but no casualties inflicted. C of E church parade 5-30 p.m. Bttn marched off at 10-15 p.m. to take up position allotted to it for tomorrows attack.	Oteh.
" Opposite Wytschaete	7/6/17		Bttn in position opposite VIERSTRAAT SWITCH at 2 a.m. Btl & Bttn Hdqrs THE FOSSE. At 3.10 a.m. (Zero hour) the mines went up, the artillery opened and attack commenced. At 8 a.m. verbal orders were received by our Hdqrs for 26th Bde Hdqrs to move up to SP13 and 7th R.H. Rifles and 2nd R. Dub. Fus. to move to the CHINESE WALL. This move was completed by 9.30 a.m. The Battalion remained in this position throughout the day, sending forward carrying parties to 8th & 9th R. Dub. Fus. on the BAVOI Line.	See Appendix I " Oteh.

Army Form C. 2118.

WAR DIARY
or
INTELLIGENCE SUMMARY.
(Erase heading not required.)

Instructions regarding War Diaries and Intelligence Summaries are contained in F. S. Regs., Part II and the Staff Manual respectively. Title pages will be prepared in manuscript.

Place	Date	Hour	Summary of Events and Information	Remarks and references to Appendices
Opposite WYTSCHAETE	8/6/17		At 4.0 a.m. the Bttn. moved forward to relieve the 47th Batn on the Black and Blue lines. Bttn. HdQrs in dug out in WYTSCHAETE WOOD. Relief complete at 7 a.m. At 11.30 a.m. Bttn. HdQrs moved to cellars in WYTSCHAETE	A.S.H.
	9/6/17		At 11.0 a.m. Lieut Inough was badly wounded in WYTSCHAETE and died a few hours later. 11 p.m. Bttn. relieved by a Bttn. of 43rd Bde. Relief complete 11.45 p.m. Bttn. moved to bivouacs in VIERSTRAAT SWITCH	A.S.H.
"	10/6/17		Bttn. remained in VIERSTRAAT SWITCH with HdQrs THE RIBB	A.S.H.
	11/6/17		Bttn. withdrawn from line and marched to CLARE CAMP.	A.S.H.
CLARE CAMP	12/6/17		Companies work Company Commanders. Capt Web proceeded on special leave.	A.S.H.

Army Form C. 2118.

WAR DIARY
or
INTELLIGENCE SUMMARY.

(Erase heading not required.)

Map ref Sheet 27 1/40000

Place	Date	Hour	Summary of Events and Information	Remarks and references to Appendices
On march	13/6/17		At 5.0am Bttn marched to billets in MERRIS AREA. Bttn Hdqrs ROUGE CROIX.	
ROUGE CROIX	14/6/17		Special parade for first foot transport at 4.45 a.m. Companies under Company arrangements throughout the day. Inspection of Bttn and Bttn transport at 11.0am by Brig Gen F. Ramsey.	
ROUGE CROIX	15/6/17			
ROUGE CROIX	16/6/17		Companies at disposal of Company Commanders.	
On march	17/6/17		At 7.30 a.m. Bttn marched to camp in WESTOUTRE	
On march	18/6/17		At 6.0 a.m. Bttn returned to billets in the MERRIS AREA with Bttn Hdqrs at ROUGE CROIX	

Army Form C. 2118.

WAR DIARY
or
INTELLIGENCE SUMMARY.

(Erase heading not required.)

Instructions regarding War Diaries and Intelligence Summaries are contained in F.S. Regs., Part II. and the Staff Manual respectively. Title pages will be prepared in manuscript.

Hohat
Sheet 27 (7040)

Place	Date	Hour	Summary of Events and Information	Remarks and references to Appendices
CROIX ROUGE	19/6/17		Companies under Company Commanders	AAA
On march	20/6/17		Bttn. moved to camp near STEENVOORDE at 5.30 a.m.	AAA
STEENVOORDE	21/6/17		Inspection by G.O.C. 48th Bde. of all who to be referred since 15th June. 2/Lt Hartley proceeded on 10 days & 91 leave.	AAA
On march	22/6/17		At 6.30 a.m. Bttn. marched to billets in the RUBROUCK Training Area. Bttn. Arrived at RUBROUCK. 16th Division was transferred from 9th Corps 2nd army to 19th Corps.	AAA
RUBROUCK	23/6/17		Company Training.	AAA

WAR DIARY or INTELLIGENCE SUMMARY

Army Form C. 2118.

Sheet 27

Place	Date	Hour	Summary of Events and Information	Remarks and references to Appendices
RoBlove R	24/6/17		Church parade. Capt Heath returned from leave	
RoBRovil	25/6/17	10.40 am	Inspection of special details by G.O.C 48th Bde (Prov.) At inspection by G.O.C. 19th Corps on 27th inst.	
"	26/6/17		Company training	
"	27/6/17		Inspection of the Mule of B'tn at training by G.O.C XIX Corps	
"	28/6/17		Special detachments from Battalion were inspected by the Corps Commander (Lt Gen H.E. WATTS CB (MG). CAPT W A Melrose and 2nd Lieut W Owens rejoined Battalion	
"	29/6/17		HQrs Cy & B Cy had Baths.	

Place	Date	Hour	Summary of Events and Information	Remarks and references to Appendices
RUBROUCK	30-6-17		Coy training as usual. Nothing to report. Strength of Battalion on 1st June 1917 40 Officers + 940 Other Ranks Strength of Battalion on 30th June 1917 39 Officers + 969 Other Ranks	
	1-7-17			

(Sd) T Roggendorff Major
O.C. 7th Royal Irish Rifles

Secret. 7th (S) Bn Royal Irish Rifles.
                Order No 118.
Ref. Sheets S.W. 1/20,000.   June 6th 1917.

1. The 7th Royal Irish Rifles will move to position of assembly as detailed in Provisional Operation Instructions on the night of 7th June 1917
2. The first Company will leave Blare Camp at 9-20 p.m.
Order of March.   B, A, D, Hdqrs + C Coy.
Route. "A" track to Soere - La Blytte Rd. (keeping to South where track branches) "Green Track" to Soere Kemmel Rd near Kemmel Shelters thence via Kemmel Church Suicide-Rd to position of assembly.
Route should be reconnitred carefully by daylight.
The Battalion must be clear of Blare Camp by 9-30 p.m. must be clear of Soere - La Blytte Rd by 10-30 p.m. + must not cross York Rd before 11-30 p.m. All troops to be in position by 2 p.m.
All movement East of Soere-La Blytte Rd is to be by platoons at 200 yds interval.
3. Whilst moving to assembly position & when finally in position, every care is to be taken to avoid arousing the suspicions of the enemy. Smoking, striking of matches, flashing of torches + unnecessary talking are forbidden.

All ranks will move as quietly as possible.
4. There will be one limber for Lewis Gun Magazines, half a limber for Medical Offr & half a limber for "D" Coy's Yukon Packs.
5. The valese instead of the haversack will be carried. All surplus kit & Officers kits will be stacked ready to be removed to Transport Lines at 4.p.m. 6th inst.
6. The wiring party of 8 men per Coy will report to 2/Lt. Maguire at Bn Hdqrs ready to proceed at 9 p.m. He will march his party with D Coy & take up a position along within them ready to proceed when called on.
7. All ranks who are remaining behind will move into camp vacated by 2nd Dubs. These will parade by companies at 9 p.m. Men detailed to remain behind as Bn Hdqrs will parade under C.S.M. D'Authreau at 9 p.m. at Orderly Room. Lt. W.J.B. Wilson will arrange for the billeting of these parties.
8. Acknowledge.

     (Sd) J.S. Steele. Captain.
   Adj. 7th.(S) Bn Royal Irish Rifles.

Copy 1 retained   5 D Coy.   9 Int Off.   13 9th Dubs.
 2 A Coy.   6 2 i/c.   10 2nd in Comm   14 48th Bde.
 3 B Coy.   7 T.O.   11 2nd Dubs   15 R.S.M.
 4 C Coy   8 Sig Off.   12 8th Dubs.   16. Med Off.
             17. Lg Off.

19. **Information.** It is extremely important to keep Hdqrs informed as to the situation. Frequent reports should be sent in. Negative information is always valuable.

20. **Liaison.** Close liaison must be kept with all Troops working in front & on the flanks.

21. Acknowledge.

        (sd) J.S. Steele. Captain.
        Adj. 7th (S) Bn Royal Irish Rifles.

Copy 1 + 2 Retained.   11. 48th Bde.
    3 C.O.   12. Sig. Off.
    4 A coy.   13. Int. Off.
    5 B coy.   14. M.G. Off.
    6 C coy.   15. S.G. Off.
    7 D coy.   16. 2nd Dubs.
    8 2M.   17. 8th Dubs.
    9 T.O   18. 9th Dubs.
  10 2nd in comdg.   19. Medl. Off.
        20. R.S.M.

Secret.   7th.(S) Bn Royal Irish Rifles.
    Provisional Operation Instructions.
Ref Wytschaete 1/10,000 Edition 5A.   5th June 1917.

1. The 2nd Army will assume the Offensive on the 7th June 1917.
2. The attack of the 16th Divn is divided into two phases + an intermediate phase.
   1st Phase. The capture of the Wytschaete Ridge (Black Line.) This task is allotted to the 47th Inf Bde (Right Bde) + the 49th Inf. Bde (Left Bde).
   Intermediate Phase. The capture of the Oil Trench (Mauve Line). To the 48th Inf. Bde is allotted this task.
   2nd Phase. The capture of the Oostaverne Line (Dk Green Line). To the 33rd Inf Bde detached from the 11th Div. is allotted this task.
3. The assault on the Oil Trench (Mauve Line) will be carried out by the 9th Royal Dub. Fus. on the Right + the 8th Royal Dub. Fus on the left. The 7th. R. I. Rifles + the 2nd R.D. Fus will be in Brigade Support on the Right + Left respectively, + will be prepared to carry forward material, water etc, for the assaulting Battalions.
4. In the event of the 9th R. D. Fus. being called upon by the G.O.C. 47th Inf. Bde + their becoming heavily engaged in the fight the 7th R.I. Rifles will become the

Right assaulting Battalion. Similiarly in the event of the 8th R.D.Fus. being sent to the assistance of the 49th Inf. Bde. the 2nd R.D.Fus. will become the Left assaulting Battalion.

5. Dispositions prior to the attack.
9th Royal Dub. Fus. Chinese Wall Line Hong Kong Section, Hdqrs at Irish House Dugouts.
8th Royal Dub. Fus. Chinese Wall Line, Pekin Section Hdqrs at S.P.13.
7th Royal Irish Rifles. Vierstraat Switch South of Desinet Farm. Hdqrs at the Fosse.
2nd Royal Dub. Fus. Vierstraat Switch North of Desinet Farm. Hdqrs at Fosse.
Brigade Hdqrs.   The Fosse.

6. The 7th R.I. Rifles will be disposed as follows:
A Coy. In ditches between Via Gellia & Rossignol Alston House.
B Coy. In ditches between Rossignol Rd & the Overland Route & West of a line running North & South through Fort Mount Royal.
C Coy. In Raven Trench & the vicinity.
D Coy. In Stork Trench & the vicinity.

7. On receipt of orders to advance the assaulting Battalions will leave the Chinese Wall timing their rate of advance so as to reach the Blue Line at zero plus 4-30 Right Battalion moving via Nap Drive,

Left Battalion moving via Nuna Drive. As soon as the Black Line is captured (Zero plus 4.40) the assaulting Battalions will move into positions of assembly as follows.

Right Battalion. The junction of Occasion Trench & Occasion Alley (West of Church)
Left Battalion. The dead ground immediately West of junction of Obvious Avenue & Obvious Trench.

8. At Zero plus 5.30 the standing barrage in front of the Black Line will advance at the rate 100 yds in 3 minutes to a line 300 yds beyond the Mauve Line where it will remain until zero plus 6.30 when it will cease unless recalled by S.O.S.

9. Assaulting Battalions will advance in depth (each on a company frontage, with 1 coy in Support & 1 coy in Reserve, the fourth coy finding Moppers up & barriers) on to the Mauve Line preceded by skirmishing Patrols with Lewis Guns: these will keep as close to the barrage as possible.

10. On reaching the Mauve Line the leading coy will throw out Trench out posts & consolidate rapidly. As much wire as possible must be got out. Support & Reserve coys will dig & wire Support &

Reserve Trenches in Rear.

11. Strong Points will be constructed by 155 Coy R.E. as follows:- (1) At the Southern end of Lig Copse with a Machine Gun placed to sweep the valley of the Wambeek + one to command ground South of Oostaverne Wood.

(2) Near Torreken Farm with a Machine Gun placed to command the valley in the direction of Oostaverne.

12. <u>Tools for Consolidation.</u> Two companies of each of the assaulting Battalions will carry tools as under:-
<u>Each Company.</u> 100 shovels + 30 picks
These tools will be drawn from dumps at Chinese Wall by the 8th + 9th R.D.Fus. In the event of the 9th R.D.Fus being involved in the Operations prior to the attack on the Mauve line these tools will be dumped at Wood Post for the use of 7th. R.I. Rifles.

13. One Section of Tanks will co-operate on either flank of the Assaulting troops.

14. Aeroplane contact patrols for 16th. Div. will be marked by a black flag attached to the Rear of each lower plane. Aeroplanes will call for flares + Watson fans by sounding a Klaxon Horn + firing a Very Light, or by either of these two signals.

Aeroplane code call for 48th Inf. Bde is
O.4 for Battalion T.W.

15. Bn Hdqrs will move from the Horse to
S.P.13 at zero plus 4. An advanced Bde
Hdqrs will open at Northouse at zero plus
4.30. Should the 7th R.S. Rifles become
the assaulting Battalion. Report centre
will be with the Reserve coy until the
Black Line is reached when it will
remain in that vicinity.

16. The Medical Officer will make the
necessary Medical arrangements &
will keep Bn Hdqrs informed of the
position of the Aid Post.

17. <u>Dress & Equipment.</u> Dress Field Service
Order.
Each man except No 1 & 2 of Lewis Guns
will carry two bombs, 150 rounds S.A.A.
& 2 sandbags. Rifle bombing sections
will carry 25 Mills Rifle bombs in
addition. Bombing sections will
carry ten Mills bombs per man
D Coy will be issued with 21 Yukon
Packs for carrying stores.

18. <u>Water & Rations.</u> All ranks are
cautioned to husband very carefully
their rations & water as the difficulty
of replenishing supplies will be very
great. One day's rations will be carried
in addition to the Iron Ration.

48/76

WAR DIARY.

FOR MONTH OF JULY, 1917.

VOLUME:- 20

UNIT:- 7th (S) Btn Royal Irish Rifles.

To 49th Bde 23/8/17

Army Form C. 2118.

WAR DIARY
or
INTELLIGENCE SUMMARY.
(Erase heading not required.)

Ref. HAZEBROUCK 5a 1/40,000

Place	Date	Hour	Summary of Events and Information	Remarks and references to Appendices
RUBROUCK	1-7-17		Church Parade. C Coy had Sports during the afternoon	-
"	2-7-17		Coy training as usual. 2nd Li Hill sick	-
"	3-7-17		B Coy had sports during the afternoon.	-
"	4-7-17		Coy training as usual.	-
"	5-7-17		Battalion sports were held for day - very successful. Result 1 Coy Championship. B Coy 17 points; C + D Coys each 13 points; A + HQ Coy 8 points each. 2 Lt P.J. Hurley returned from leave.	-
"	6-7-17		2nd Lieut R. Grace reported for duty & posted to B Coy.	-
"	7-7-17		Services were held instead of 8th inst.	-
"	8-7-17		Battalion moved from RUBROUCK area to billets in TILQUES training area. HQrs + A Coy are in CORMETTE; B, C + D Coys in AUDENFUM. No men fell out on march. Route ST OMER, ST MARTIN AU LAERT.	-
"	9-7-17		Companies carried out training during the afternoon.	-

Army Form C. 2118.

WAR DIARY
or
INTELLIGENCE SUMMARY.

(Erase heading not required.)

Instructions regarding War Diaries and Intelligence Summaries are contained in F.S. Regs., Part II. and the Staff Manual respectively. Title pages will be prepared in manuscript.

Place	Date	Hour	Summary of Events and Information	Remarks and references to Appendices
CORMETTE	10-7-17		Lieut William Barrett reported for duty as 8th Lieut and took over duties of Quartermaster. Lieut C.P. Francis R.A.M.C. returned from 48th Inf Bde. The Battalion carried out Battalion training in the Training area. 2nd Lt K.K. Pelton M.C. returned from leave.	JH
"	11-7-17		Bde exercise was carried out during the afternoon (see other attached.)	
"	12-7-17		Battalion fired on "A" Range MOVILLE from 4am - 12 noon. 2nd Lt K.K. Pelton returned from leave.	JH
"	13-7-17		Rehearsal of Bde Exercise which the carried out on 14th inst	JH
"	14-7-17		2nd Lt ACD Hill proceeded on leave. Bde Exercise started at 8am. Rain commenced at 8:30 am - Bn marched home soon after	JH
"	15-7-17		Church parades. R.C. Church parade in ST OMER.	JH
"	16-7-17		Bn. moved from CORMETTE to ZAGGERS CAPEL (see new whereby) Lieut Kingston proceeded on leave. Bn. billetted in new area.	JH

Army Form C. 2118.

WAR DIARY
or
INTELLIGENCE SUMMARY.

(Erase heading not required.)

1/4th Bn. KRRC No. 5a 100,000

Place	Date	Hour	Summary of Events and Information	Remarks and references to Appendices
ZAGGERS CAPPEL	17/7/17		Coy training. 2nd Lieut M.J. Harting awarded the M.C. 4081 CSM. A/RSM Le Breton awarded D.C.M. 2nd Lieut V.C. Young proceeded on leave.	ff
"	18-7-17		Major Rigg awarded the Croix de Guerre.	ff
"	19-7-17		Inspection by Army Commander (General Gough). Transport inspected at training and Companies were inspected at training.	ff
"	20-7-17		Coy training.	ff
"	21-7-17		Coy training.	ff
CAMP WIMEZEELE	22-7-17		Battalion marched as part of the 48th Inf Bde to Camp near WIMEZEELE. All Battalion in one field.	ff
"	23-7-17		Reconnaissance of 15th Div area carried out by Commanding Officer, Adjutant, O.C.Coy's, O.T.O.G. and Supply Officer.	ff

Army Form C. 2118.

WAR DIARY
or
INTELLIGENCE SUMMARY.

(Erase heading not required.)

A2E BROWN Sa 100, 117, and 28 tg 117

Place	Date	Hour	Summary of Events and Information	Remarks and references to Appendices
CAMP WINEZEELE	24-7-17		Divisional Commander had a Ribbon Decoration Ceremony for Officers + other Ranks who had not yet been invested. D Coy attended the ceremony.	AA
CAMP WATOU AREA No 1	25/7/17		Battalion marched from Camp near WINEZEELE. Left at 5.10 a.m. arrived here about 10 a.m. Near POPERINGHE. Major Rigg, Major Allan and Capt McMaster proceeded to remount 15th Div. Front.	AA
	26/7/17 to 29/7/17		In Camp. Company training. Lt Hill returned from leave 27th inst. Lt Rupston " " 28th inst. 2nd Lt Boyle proceeded on leave 26th inst.	AA
TORONTO CAMP J 18 d 5.7	30-7-17	10 pm	Bn. marched to TORONTO CAMP where it is in a Position of readiness in Corps Reserve. (see map No 129 attached.)	AA

WAR DIARY
or
INTELLIGENCE SUMMARY

Army Form C. 2118.

Place: Trench
Date: 31/7/17
Hour: —

At 11 p.m. on the 30th inst the Battalion was in a position of Readiness in Corps reserve at G.18 a 5.7. At 3:40 a.m. totaling the Battle commenced. At 4:30 a.m. the Batt. less details and Transport moved to a Position of Assembly at H.16.a. This position was reached at 7 a.m. Companies were distributed in lodges. The Batt. remained here all day until 7:30 p.m. when it moved up to become under orders of the 154th Division. It here attacked to the 44th Inf Bde. where HQrs were at JAMES FARM at I.4.d.6.1. On arrival at Bde HQrs. Coys were put in position in depth as follows.

C Coy in CAMBRIDGE TRENCH from I.11.b.2.9 to YPRES-ROULERS RAILWAY.
D Coy from I.10 b 20.95 to Railway.
B Coy from I.4.d.2.8 to Railway YPRES ROULERS
A Coy ECOLE at I.9 c 5.2.
HQrs then C Coy about 200 yards North of ROULERS RAILWAY in position fire in Bde support at 1 a.m. 1st August 1917.

Army Form C. 2118.

WAR DIARY
or
INTELLIGENCE SUMMARY.
(Erase heading not required.)

Place	Date	Hour	Summary of Events and Information	Remarks and references to Appendices
TRENCHES	31-7-17		No Casualties during the day.	
			Strength at commencement of month. 37 Officers and 951 Other Ranks.	
			Strength Today. 36 Officers & 857 Other Ranks.	

[signatures]

2/8/17

SECRET.   7th (S) Bn Royal Irish Rifles.   Copy No.........

O R D E R   N O   1 2 4.

Ref Hazebrouck 5 a. 1/100,000.   Saturday 7th July 1917.

1. The Battalion will move to billets at CORMETTE, AUDENTHUM and LEULINE on the 8th July 1917.
2. Companies will form up in threes on the RUBROUCK-BROXEELE road facing WEST ready to move off at 4-45 a.m.
   Head of column will be 50 yards EAST of Cross Roads 300 yards WEST of RUBROUCK CHURCH.
   Order of Companies. Hdqrs, A, B, C, D.
3. March discipline will be strictly enforced.
   2/Lieut R.A.J.Thompson will be in command of the Police and Bombers who will be the rear party.
   List of men falling out will be sent to Battalion Headquarters by 2/Lieut Thompson 2 hours after arrival in billets.
4. Every man falling out on line of march will be provided with a slip signed by an officer.
5. Packs will be carried on the march.
6. Acknowledge.

                            Captain.
       Adjutant 7th (S) Bn Royal Irish Rifles.

Copy No 1 & 2 retained.
       3 A Coy.
       4 B Coy.
       5 C Coy.
       6 D Coy.
       7 Q.M.
       8 T.Offr.
       9. 48th Bde.
      10. Sig.Offr.
      11. Int.Offr.
      12. 9th Dublins.
      13. R.S.M.
      14. 2nd inCom.
      15. 2nd Dublins.
      16. Med.Offr.

7th (S) Bn Royal Irish Rifles.

ORDER NO 1/5.

Ref Sheet 27 a S.E. 1/20,000   10th July 1917.

1. The 48th Infantry Brigade will carry out a Tactical Exercise on 11th July 1917.
2. There will be three objectives.
   - 1st. Blue Line.
   - 2nd. Green Line.) as shown on attached maps.
   - 3rd. Brown Line.
3. The 7th Irish Rifles, (Left Battalion) and 9th R.Dub.Fus (Right Battalion) will be in position of readiness on the red line at ZERO minus 30 minutes.
   The 8th R.Dub.Fus. and 2nd R.D.Fus in Position of Assembly in valley immediately in rear.
4. The Battalion will attack on a **2** Coy front.
   C & D Coys in Front Line. A & B Coys in Support.
   C Coy. RIGHT.   A Coy in rear of C Coy.
   D Coy. LEFT.   B Coy in rear of D Coy.
   No carrying company will be required.
5. The successive phases of the attack will be carried out under cover of an Artillery and Machine Gun Barrage. This Artillery Barrage will be represented by Infantry carrying red flags and drums.
6. At ZERO hour the 7th Irish Rifles and 9th R.D.Fus will advance to assault of Blue Line.
   A halt of 10 minutes will be made on the Blue Line and the advance then continued to Green Line which will be reached at ZERO plus **40** minutes.
   This Line will be consolidated and wired.
7. At ZERO plus **100** minutes the 8th R.D.Fus. and 2nd R.D.Fus. will cross the Green Line and establish themselves on the Brown Line.
8. Battalion Headquarters will be at W.4.b.5.9. until the capture of the Green Line when it will move to W.11.b.2.7.
9. Zero hour will be at **2** p.m.
10. The Battalion Commander will meet Company Commanders mounted at Cross roads at W.4.a.7.3. at **9** a.m. 11th inst.

Captain.
Adjutant 7th (S) Bn Royal Irish Rifles.

Copy No 1 & 2 retained.
3 A Coy.
4 B Coy.
5 C Coy.
6 D Coy.
7 Q.M.
8. Transport Offr.
9. Sig. Offr.
10. Int. Offr.
11. Stokes Gun Offr.
12. R.S.M.
13. M.G.Offr.
14. 48th Bde.
15. Med.Offr.
16. 2nd in Com.

7th (S) Bn Royal Irish Rifles.

ORDER NO 135. (For training purposes).
Ref Sheet 27.a.S.E. 1/20,000.   15th July 1917.

1. On the 14th inst, in accordance with General and Special Idea already issued the 48th Inf Brigade will attack on a 2 Battalion front with 2 Battalions in Support.
Each Battalion will attack in depth on a two Company front.
2. To the 8th R.Dub.Fus on right and 7th Irish Rifles on left is allotted the capture of the BLUE & GREEN LINES.
3. The 7th Irish Rifles will be in a position of readiness behind the RED LINE at ZERO minus 30 minutes.

   C Coy. Right Front Coy.   A & B Coys in rear of C & D Coys
   D Coy. Left Front Coy.   respectively.
   Battalion Headquarters at W.4.b.5.9.

4. At ZERO hour the Battalion will advance under cover of a creeping barrage which will move at the rate of 100 yds in 4 minutes.
5. The BLUE LINE will be reached at ZERO plus 40 minutes and will be immediately consolidated.
Officers Commanding A & B Coys will each send forward 1 platoon to construct & garrison strong points at positions to be indicated by Officers Commanding Coys in the front line.
6. (a). At ZERO plus 70 minutes the advance will be continued to the GREEN LINE which will be reached at ZERO plus 100 mins. A defensive line will be immediately constructed and wired.
6. (b). A Coy less 1 platoon and B Coy less 1 platoon will take up a position in close support of the GREEN LINE each detailing 1 platoon to carry forward wire and report to Officers Commanding C & D Coys respectively who will indicate the front to be wired.
7. At ZERO plus 130 minutes the 2nd R.Dub.Fus. and 8th R.D.Fus. will cross the GREEN LINE and advance to final objective.
8. Forward Dumps for Ammunition, tools, water and wire will be established at W.4.d.8.2. and W.11.b.2.8. by Pack train.
A & B Coys will supply carrying parties to front line from these dumps.
9. One section Trench Mortar Battery will accompany the Battalion and will advance in rear of and between C & D Coys. Each Coy will detail 6 men to report to the Officer Commdg. this T.M.Section at ZERO minus 30 minutes.
10. 2 Vickers Guns will accompany the Battalion and will march in rear of and between A & B Coys.
On capture of GREEN LINE they will take up a position to form a belt of fire and to cover the advance to the final objective.
11. On capture of BLUE LINE Battalion Hdqrs will move to W.5.c.2.8.   On capture of GREEN LINE they will move to W. 11.a.9.5. where all reports will be sent.
12. S.O.S. Call.   A single Red Rocket.
13. Companies will synchronize watches at Battalion Headquarters at ZERO minus 20 minutes.
14. ZERO hour. 8 a.m.

                                  Captain.
      Adjutant 7th (S) Bn Royal Irish Rifles.

Copies 1 & 2 retained. 3 A Coy 4 B Coy 5 C Coy 6 D Coy.
      7 Quartermaster 8 Transport Officer 9 48th Brigade.
      10. Sig.Offr.   11.Int.Offr.   12. Med.Offr.
      13. T.M.Offr.   14.M.G.Offr.   15. R.S.M.
      16. 2nd in Com. 17. Commanding Officer. 18 War Diary.

SECRET. 7th (S) Bn Royal Irish Rifles. Copy No. A...

O R D E R N O 126.

Ref. Sheet 27 a. S.E. 1/30,000 & Hazebrouck 5 a 1/100,000.
In the Field.   Sunday 15th July 1917.

---

1. The Battalion will move to billets in the ERINGHEM AREA on the 16th inst.

2. Order of march will be Hdqrs, B Coy, C Coy, D Coy, A Coy. and Transport. The head of column will pass the CROSS ROADS at LONGUEBORNE (Q.35.d.95.55). at 5-10 a.m.

3. 2/Lieut H.H. Hoops will be in charge of the police and bombers who will be the rear party. List of men falling out will be sent to Batt. Hdqrs by 2/Lt H.H. Hoops 2 hours after arrival of Battalion in billets.

4. Every man falling out on line of march will be provided with a slip signed by an officer.

5. Officers valises of B, C & D Coys will be stacked at the Quartermasters Stores by 4-15 a.m.
Hdqrs and A Coy officers valises will be loaded at Orderly Room by 4 a.m.

6. A rear party of 1 N.C.O. and 3 men per Company will remain behind to clean up billets. These parties will march to new billets under 2/Lieut xxxxxxx M.J. Woulfe.

                                              Captain.
            Adjutant 7th (S) Bn Royal Irish Rifles.

Copy No 1 & 2 retained.
        3 A Coy.
        4 B Coy.
        5 C Coy.
        6 D Coy.
        7 Quartermaster.
        8. Transport Officer.
        9. 48th Inf. Bde.
        10. Signal Officer.
        11. Intelligence Officer.
        12. R.S.M.
        13. Second in Command.
        14. Medical Officer.
        15. War Diary.
        16. Commanding Officer.

SECRET.   7th (S) Bn ROYAL IRISH RIFLES.   Copy No. 2

ORDER NO 137.

In the Field.   21st July 1917.

1. The Battalion will move to No 3 Area WINNEZEELE to-morrow 22nd July 1917 and will be camped at J.2.b.2.9. Advanced parties have left to-day.

2. Order of March.
   A and D Coys will be formed up in that order on road opposite A Coy and Hdqrs billet at 6-50 a.m.
   C and B Coys and Transport will be formed up in that order on road South of Railway with head of column South of Railway Crossing at 6-50 a.m.
   DRESS.   Marching Order with packs.

3. Officers valises will be stacked outside Coy and Bn Hdqrs at 5 a.m. and will be collected by baggage wagon.

4. Billets must be thoroughly clean and inspected by an officer before marching off. No rear parties will be left.

5. 2/Lieut Beatty will report to Brigade Headquarters at head of column at 6-40 a.m. He will be mounted and will proceed the column accompanied by 4 Mounted Police for the purpose of blocking roads and giving warning to Control Posts.

6. The Police and Battalion Bombers under 2/Lieut HATTE will march in rear of the Battalion and will pick up stragglers. List of men falling out will be sent to Battalion Headquarters on arrival in camp.

7. One guide for Supply Wagons to be at Refilling Point at LES TROIS BOIS (J.8.a.6.2) at 11 a.m. 22nd inst.

                                                    2/Lieut.
                        A/Adjutant 7th (S) Bn Royal Irish Rifles.

Copy No 1 & 2 retained   3 War Diary.
         4 A Coy.
         5 B Coy.
         6 C Coy.
         7 D Coy
         8. Quartermaster.
         9 Transport Officer.
        10 Signalling Officer.
        11. Intelligence Officer.
        12. 48th Inf.Bde.
        13. R.S.M.
        14. Med. Offr.
        15. 2nd in Com.
        16. Commanding Officer.

SECRET.   7th (S) Bn ROYAL IRISH RIFLES.   Copy No......

O R D E R N O 12

In the Field.   24th July 1917.
Ref Sheet 27 L/40.000.

1. The Battalion will march to WATOU No 1 Area on July 25'17.

2. Companies will form up ready to march off at 5-10 a.m.
   Order of March.   Hdqrs, C Coy, A Coy, B Coy, D Coy. Transport.
   Dress.   Fighting Order with steel helmets carried
                     on haversack.

3. Officers valises will be stacked at Q.M.Stores at 4 a.m.

4. Billets must be thoroughly clean and inspected by an
   officer before marching off. No rear parties will be left.
   The Police and Battalion Bombers under 2/Lt K.K.Pelton M.C.
   will march in rear of the Battalion and will pick up
   stragglers. List of men falling out will be sent to
   Battalion Headquarters on arrival in camp.

5. Refilling point on 25th inst will be at L.15.B.5.5.

6. All packs will be stacked by Companies at Q.M.Stores
   by 4 a.m. 25th inst.

7. Acknowledge.

                                              Captain.
                          Adjutant 7th (S) Bn Royal Irish Rifles.

Copy No 1 & 2 retained.   3. War Diary.
        4 A Coy.
        5 B Coy.
        6 C Coy.
        7 D Coy.
        8. Quartermaster.
        9. Transport Officer.
       10. Signalling Officer.
       11. Intelligence Officer.
       12. 48th Inf. Bde.
       13. R.S.M.
       14. Medical Officer.
       15. 2nd in Command.
       16. Commanding Officer.

SECRET.   7th (S) Bn ROYAL IRISH RIFLES.   Copy No. 3

O R D E R   N O 127.

Ref Sheet 28 N.W. 1/20,000.   30th July 1917.

1. The Battalion will move to position of READINESS at TORONTO CAMP.G.10.a.5.7. this evening July 30th 17, and will move from thence to ASSEMBLY POSITION in H.18.a. at a time to be notified later.

2. The Battalion will be ready to march off at 8 p.m. in the order Hdqrs, C, D, A & B Coys.
Two hundred yards distance between Companies WEST of VLAMERTINGHE and Two hundred yards between platoons EAST of VLAMERTINGHE.
DRESS. Fighting Order with packs; no greatcoats or haversacks.

3. Iron Ration and one days full ration will be carried in the pack. One days full ration on the cooker.

4. The following will be drawn at position of READINESS
To be carried in the pack.) 50 rounds S.A.A. per man.
) 2 Bombs per man.

To be carried behind the pack) 30 picks and shovels per
) Coy except A Coy.
Men carrying picks and shovels will not carry entrenching implements.

5. All ranks detailed to remain behind will be left at position of READINESS.

6. Kits will be conveyed by lorry to position of READINESS at 10 a.m. to-day. Officers kits will be loaded on Baggage Wagon by 7 p.m. to-day.

7. All transport will accompany Battalion to position of READINESS. Cookers and Water Carts will accompany Battalion to position of ASSEMBLY.

8. On arrival at position of ASSEMBLY every precaution will be taken to conceal troops from enemy observation.
Sentries will be posted by Companies and provided with whistles to give warning of approach of hostile aeroplanes.

                                            Captain.
              Adjutant 7th (S) Bn Royal Irish Rifles.

Copies 1 & 2 retained 3 War Diary.
       4 A Coy.   5 B Coy.   6 C Coy.   7 D Coy.
       8 Quartermaster.
       9 Transport Officer.
      10. 48th Inf.Bde.
      11. Signalling Officer.
      12. Int. Officer.
      13. R.S.M.
      14. Second in Command
      15. Medical Officer
      16. Commanding Officer

49/16.

WAR DIARY.

FOR MONTH OF AUGUST, 1917.

VOLUME............

UNIT 7th Royal Irish Rifles

Came from 8th Bn 27.8.17.

Aug 17

WAR DIARY
INTELLIGENCE SUMMARY

August 1917

28 NW. 20,000

Place	Date	Hour	Summary of Events and Information	Remarks and references to Appendices
Trenches	1-8-17		At 1 a.m. the Bn was in position in Bde Reserve to the 44th Bde.	
			At 4:30 p.m. a message was received to send 5 guides to meet 7th Lunatics who were to relieve us. Guides were to be at MENIN GATE at 5 p.m. Guides were immediately despatched.	
			At 6 p.m. a message was received to the effect that we would not be relieved by the 7th Lunatics until the situation in front was cleaner. At the same time an order was received to stand to and be ready to hold old German front system. It was believed that the Enemy had broken through NORTH of FROST HOUSE.	
			At 7:15 p.m. a message was received to carry on with the relief. We were not however to withdraw when relieved without orders of 15th Div. The 7th Lunatics arrived at 8 p.m. and relief was reported complete.	

Army Form C. 2118.

WAR DIARY
or
INTELLIGENCE SUMMARY.

(Erase heading not required.)

Sheet 28 NW 20,000

Place	Date	Hour	Summary of Events and Information	Remarks and references to Appendices
TORONTO CAMP G.18.a.5.7.	2-8-17		At 2:15 a.m. an order was received from 44th Inf. Bde. The 7th Lunatics were to occupy all strong points on BLUE LINE. We were to remain. The Lunatics moved at 3 a.m. At 4 a.m. a message was received to send guides to meet a Batt. of 47th Bde who were to relieve us. No guides were sent to POTIJZE CHATEAU but no Batt. turned up. At 2:10 p.m. a message was received from A/Staff Capt 44th Inf. Bde to march to ASYLUM H.12.d. and there entrain for G.11.c.9.7. The Bn. marched back, entrained, left the ASYLUM at 6:30 p.m. arrived at BRAND HOEK and marched to G.18.a.5.7. (TORONTO CAMP.) Arrived there at 7:15 p.m. 2 Casualties in Battalion. 2nd Lieut K.T. PELTON & 4 Lunatics att. to us was killed on 1-8-17 whilst attached to Bde for intelligence work.	

A-5834 Wt. W4973/M687 750,000 8/16 D. D. & L. Ltd. Forms/C.2118/13.

Army Form C. 2118.

WAR DIARY
or
INTELLIGENCE SUMMARY.

(Erase heading not required.)

N.W 30m + 28 NE

Place	Date	Hour	Summary of Events and Information	Remarks and references to Appendices
TORONTO CAMP	3-8-17		Rested all day. Had Baths during the morning.	A/A
"	4-8-17		Rested all day.	A/A
ÉCOLE YPRES	5-8-17		Marched to Railway near BRANDHOEK - entrained here - detrained at ASYLUM YPRES - marched to ECOLE and relieved 7/8th R. IR. Irs. (see order 130)	A/A
"	6-8-17		Heavily shelled but had very few casualties	
FREEZEN BERG	7-8-17		The Battalion moved to the front line and relieved the 2nd R. Dub. Fus. A Coy in FREEZEN BERG REDOUBT B Coy in Support Right on ROULERS - YPRES RAILWAY	

Army Form C. 2118.

WAR DIARY
or
INTELLIGENCE SUMMARY.

(Erase heading not required.)

Sheet 28 NW & NE 1/20,000

Place	Date	Hour	Summary of Events and Information	Remarks and references to Appendices
FREEZEN-BERG	7-8-17		C Coy in front line Right in Railway. D Coy in front line on left of C Coy. Bn HQrs in FREEZENBERG REDOUBT. Very dark coming up. Heavy shelling several casualties.	JH
"	8-8-17		Intermittent shelling during the day. Bn HQrs were hit and all the runners and Narrows either killed or wounded.	JH
"	9-8-17		Major H.S. Allison killed. 2nd Lt J. P. Roche wounded both of B Coy.	JH
Camp at HIS FL 8	10-8-17		The Batt was relieved in the night 9/10th by 8th R Dub. Fus and on completion of relief returned to camp at HIS FL 8. Casualties from 6-10th were 12 killed. 75 wounded. missing 4	JH

Army Form C. 2118.

WAR DIARY
or
INTELLIGENCE SUMMARY.
(Erase heading not required.)

Army: 2 ANE to 20 DD

Place	Date	Hour	Summary of Events and Information	Remarks and references to Appendices
VIERSTRAAT H.E.	10/8/17 to 14/8/17		In Bde Reserve, resting and preparing for a Mine. Found HQ. Capt Malone rejoined on 13th. Draft from Corps Reinforcement Depot. Capt Hope Carson proceeded to take his place.	HH
Trenches	15/8/17		The Batt. moved forward into Assembly position (one attached orders) at 7pm and had got into position by 2.30 a.m. 16/8/17.	HH

WAR DIARY
INTELLIGENCE SUMMARY

Army Form C. 2118.

Place	Date	Hour	Summary of Events and Information	Remarks and references to Appendices
28 NE 23.07	16-8-17		Arrived assembly position at 2.25 am. No tape had been put out by R.E. Any further excellent arrangements made by Capt Black & the Officers of "A" Coy 2" R. Dub. Fus. the Batt. had no difficulty in getting into position. Some casualties had occurred on the way up from shell fire. One direct hit on MENIN GATE wounded several men of STORES MULES Party. At about 4 am being shelled position pretty heavily. At Zero hour immediately the barrage started the enemy opened with M.Gs and shelled the BLACK LINE. During the advance to GREEN LINE many M.Gs" were active from several places in the YPRES-ROULERS RAILWAY — the direction of BORRY FARM and from cements dugouts at D26a2.0 and D26c3.7. At the latter point the fire kept in action while the barrage passed over them. Two MGs fire caused a great many casualties. All of the Mures were hit before the GREEN LINE was reached. The CENTRE & LEFT Co.Y suffered very severely and were not able to go on. The Right Coy suffered similarly	see Maps attached

WAR DIARY or INTELLIGENCE SUMMARY

Army Form C. 2118.

Place	Date	Hour	Summary of Events and Information	Remarks and references to Appendices
	16/8/17		The Huts and Dugouts at D26.C.4.5 readily took about 30 prisoners. These Sigs then moved along the Railway & across the HANEBEKE. Some of them were seen to follow the barrage to the RED DOTTED LINE. A few of the centre and support Coys seemed to have followed them though, with the exception of these few the whole line came to a standstill. An attempt was made to turn the flank of the dugouts at D26.C.3.7 from the direction of the huts. Lieut Kington was killed while leading his revolver ynmot the M.G. Crew, & what was left of his Platoon was knocked out by a shell a small party consolidated a point of the Railway near the huts. The M.G.'s firing up parts of the 2nd R.D.F. came up and gave the support of the day themselves in approximately on the line of the road at D26.C.2.7. At this time the situation was not at all clear. No message got back I was only getting scraps of information from the wounded. I had sent an Officer with 4 orderlies specially to report on the situation when the GREEN LINE was reached (2nd Lt. A.D. HELL) He has not been seen since soon after Zero hour.	

Place	Date	Hour	Summary of Events and Information	Remarks and references to Appendices
	16/8/17		At 10:15 a.m. at his own suggestion Capt Conley 8th R. Dub. Fus. took his Coy out to assist in clearing the GREEN LINE. He appeared about D.26.c.1.9. determined not to make any progress. At this stage I found that the Casualties had been so heavy that it was not possible to advance in face of the Machine Gun fire. The Rest. on our right had also been held up, but we kept in touch with them at the Ando on the GREEN LINE that ran with them kept held up at VAN MAE FARM. Twas not possible to get any message back from the scattered parties who had got forward & were two men round & they were cut off later in the afternoon by enemy from the direction of ZONNEBEKE. At 4.0 p.m. the enemy were observed advancing at ZEVENKOTE from WINDMILL CABARET & on D.2 entered from N.E. At the same time strong parties were seen just south of the railway & west of ZONNEBEKE. At about 4.10 p.m. the Battn. on the right retired past the black line. D.5 had very few men left and 5 men from Stokes Coy under 2nd Lt were sent to form a defensive flank.	

Army Form C. 2118.

WAR DIARY
or
INTELLIGENCE SUMMARY.
(Erase heading not required.)

Place	Date	Hour	Summary of Events and Information	Remarks and references to Appendices
	16/8/17		The 2nd R.D.F. had a rough day in the BLACK line & the 2nd R.I.F. sent a Coy to assist. The enemy did not press this attack being doubtless by Artillery & machine gun fire in front of Dragoon or rather after the advance of Infantry. My hdqrs at D 26 c. 4.5. My post on the railway thus [sketch] In none of our 6 men was attacked by some enemy who advanced along south side of railway. As they were whittled to be cut off, the post retired along railway about 200 yards & took up another position. The two men who had been seen west of the HANNE BEKE were then left without a connecting post but to the join of H Sp & Artillery from left side had extended the railway I do not think any of these could have been left alive. The line on the NE West of POTSDAM DUGOUTS gradually dwindled away in casualties & the last six men with an 2nd DUBLINS came back to the BLACK LINE under cover of darkness.	[illegible initial]
	17/6/17.		The day passed quietly and relief came at dusk. The Batt. proceeded to camp by No 3 Area VLAMERTINGHE among the	

WAR DIARY
INTELLIGENCE SUMMARY

Army Form C. 2118.

Q & N E & Sheet LENS

Place	Date	Hour	Summary of Events and Information	Remarks and references to Appendices
NEAR POPERINGHE	18/8/17		About 6 a.m. 18th inst. Casualties 16th & 17th inst. 5 Officers killed, 5 wounded and 7 missing. Other ranks 39 killed & 269 wounded or missing. Entrained at VLAMERTINGHE at 3 p.m. detrained at POPERINGHE & marched to Camp at L15.b.9.1. Ref sheet 27.	JH
"	19/8/17		Day was spent quietly in Camp cleaning up & re-fitting	JH
WORMHOUDT	20/8/17		Bn. marched to WORMHOUDT en route for 3rd Army.	JH
	21/8/17		The Batt. entrained at 1:20 p.m. at ESQUELBECQ and detrained at BAPAUME at 9:30 p.m. and then marched to billets in COURCELLES coming into VI Corps 3rd Army.	JH
COURCELLES LE COMTE	22-8-17		The day passed very quietly	JH
ACHIET LE-PETIT	23-8-17		Orders were received at 8 a.m. that the Batt. was to be transferred to 49th Inf Bde. We moved from 48th Inf Bde at 5:10 p.m. Gen Ramsay gave us a farewell. Came under orders of 49th Inf Bde unbrigaded.	JH

Army Form C. 2118.

WAR DIARY
or
INTELLIGENCE SUMMARY

Maps... 2 1:10,000 & 28 NE 1:20,000

Place	Date	Hour	Summary of Events and Information	Remarks and references to Appendices
ACHIET-LE-PETIT.	24-8-17 to 27-8-17		Coy training, and refitting. Gen. Lewson-Gower inspected the Battalion on 25th inst. at 11 a.m.	
No Cm prener ERVILLERS	28/8/17		The 16th Div took over Centre sector VI Corps front. The 49th Inf Bde moved into Div Reserve. The Batt. moved from ACHIET-LE-PETIT at 10:50 am arriving in Camp at 1:15 pm.	
"	29/8/17		Remaining in Div Reserve. Companies are having Lewis Gunnery and generally re-organising for coming trench warfare.	
"	31/8/17		During the month the following Officers were killed: 2nd Lieut K.K. Pelton M.C. 1-8-17. Major H.S. Allison. 9-8-17. Major Allison is buried just in rear of FREZENBERG REDOUBT. 2nd Lt. Pelton is buried in rear of DOUGLAS VILLA.	

WAR DIARY

Army Form C. 2118.

Place	Date	Hour	Summary of Events and Information	Remarks and references to Appendices
RIVILLERS	31/8/17		The following Officers were killed during the attack on 16th Capt. C. McMaster M.C.; Lieut A.N. Oakshott; Lieut W. Kyger. 2nd Lieut Hutto. Wounded Capt J. Craig; Capt R.L. Henderson; Lieut Wyatt Whelan; 2nd Lt Beatty; 2nd Lt R. Freneau; 2nd Lt R.L. Crump; 2nd Lt M.J. Hunter (at duty). Missing 2nd Lt McFarrell, 2nd Lt W.J. Irwin; 2nd Lt J.B. C Elliott, 2nd Lt R. Howard; 2nd Lt W. Davies; 2nd Lt A. Hughes. Strength of Batt on 1-8-17. 36 Officers & 862 Other Ranks. Strength of Batt on 31-8-17. 18 Officers & 606 Other Ranks.	

S.S. Irvine
O.C. 7½ (S) Bn Royal Irish Rifles

SECRET.   7th (S) BN ROYAL IRISH RIFLES.   Copy No. 3

ORDER NO 123.

Ref Sheet 28 N.W. 1/20,000.   5th August 1917.

---

1. The line formerly held by the 13th Div will be taken over by the 48th and 49th Brigades. The 48th Brigade will be on the right.

2. The 2nd Royal Dublin Fus will relieve the 7th Leinsters in the front line (BLACK LINE).

The 8th Royal Dublin Fus will be in support in vicinity of WILDE WOOD (BLUE LINE).

The 7th Royal Irish Rifles will be accomodated in the ECOLE and SCHOOL HOUSE in relief of 7/8th R.Irish Fusiliers

3. Battalion will parade ready to march off at 2 p.m. to-day 5th inst.

DRESS and EQUIPMENT. Same as was worn when leaving this camp on 31st ult.

Two days rations will be carried and the Iron Ration.
Cookers will accompany the Battalion and will be retained at school if possible.

Two Lewis Gun Limbers will accompany the Battalion, and one for T.M. Section.

Order of March. Hdqrs, A, B, C and D Coys.

ROUTE. VLAMERTINGHE - MENIN GATE.

EAST OF VLAMERTINGHE 200 yds distance between platoons will be preserved.

4. Battalion Transport and Q.M. Stores will move to VLAMERTINGHE.No 3 AREA at H.17.C.1.5. and take over from 7th LEINSTERS.

5. Details left out of the line will parade separately and will move to Camp at G.12.d.2.4. under Major W.T.Rigg. as soon as Battalion has marched off.

6. On arrival at new position great care is to be taken that all precautions against gas are strictly observed.

7. Owing to the wet weather all the usual precautions must be taken against trench feet.

8. Acknowledge.

                                    Captain.
        Adjutant 7th (S) Bn Royal Irish Rifles.

    Copies No 1 & 2 retained. 3 War Diary.
            4 A Coy. 5 B Coy. 6 C Coy. 7 D Coy.
            8 Quartermaster.
            9. Transport Officer.
            10. Signalling Officer.
            11. Int. Officer.
            12. 48th Brigade.
            13. 2nd in Com.
            14. R.S.M.
            15. Med.Officer.
            16. Commanding Officer.

SECRET.   7th (S) BN ROYAL IRISH RIFLES.   Copy No. 3

ORDER NO 135.
14th August 1917.

Reference Sheet 1/10,000 FREZENBURG.

1. The advance will be resumed at a date and hour to be notified later.

2. At Zero hour the 7th Royal Irish Rifles will be in ASSEMBLY POSITION on tapes laid out by R.E. in rear of BLACK LINE between D.25.d.5.9. and D.25.d.3.5. Headquarters at D 25 d.4.3.
   Front Line; C, D, A Companies from Right to left in attack formation.   B Company in Support.
   9th Royal Dub. Fus. in similar formation on our left. Headquarters at D.25.d.9.8.
   2nd Royal Dub. Fus. (Support Battalion) in BLACK LINE. Headquarters. FREZENBURG REDOUBT.
   1st Royal Mun. Fus. (Reserve Battalion) in BLUE LINE.

3. To the 7th Royal Irish Rifles and 9th Royal Dub. Fus. is allotted the task of capturing and consolidating the RED DOTTED LINE from D.26.b.6.9 to D.20.c.9.3.

4. 2nd Middlesex Regt is on our Right.   Boundary. YPRES-ROULERS RAILWAY inclusive to 7th Royal Irish Rifles. 9th Royal Dub.Fus on our left.   Boundary. A line drawn from D.25.d.5.6. to Southern Edge of BOSTIN FARM.

5. The attack will be made in two bounds.
   1st Bound.   GREEN LINE. D.26.C.45.45 to D.26.a.25.10. This line will be reached at Zero plus 25 minutes. There will be a halt of 20 minutes on this line.
   2nd Bound.   At Zero plus 45 minutes the Battalion will advance to RED DOTTED LINE which will be reached at Zero plus 70 minutes.

6. The creeping barrage will advance at the rate of 100 yds in 5 minutes.
   A protective barrage will remain about 300 yds in front of RED DOTTED LINE until Zero plus 2 hours 50 minutes after which Artillery will only fire on receipt of S.O.S. Signal.

7. As soon as RED DOTTED LINE is captured, Front Line Coys will consolidate and push out patrols to edge of standing barrage.
   B Coy will pass through front line Companies and establish a Forward Strong Point at about D.26.b.8.7.
   A similar Forward Strong Point will be made by 9th Royal Dublin Fus. in BOSTIN FARM.
   One Company 2nd Royal Dub.Fus will follow the 7th Royal Irish Rifles at Zero hour and will form strong supporting points at D.25.d.75.50; D.26.C.40.45; D.26.C.35.80; and POTSDAM FARM.

8. On capture of the RED DOTTED LINE the Battalion Headquarters will move to vicinity of POTSDAM. leaving a Relay runner post in the original Headquarters.

9. 2 Stokes Guns will accompany Battalion and will follow immediately in rear of B Coy until RED DOTTED LINE is reached when they will take up positions from which they can break up a Counter-attack.

(2)

ORDER NO 133 continued.

10. 1 Section from 48th M.G.Company will follow the Battalion and take up position about D.26.b.4.3. to fire S.E.
11. A carrying Platoon of 8th Royal Dub.Fus is attached to the Battalion. It will remain under cover in vicinity of R.E.Dump at C.30.d.8.4. keeping 2 runners at FREZENBURG REDOUBT.
12. Contact Aeroplane will be marked with a BLACK PLAQUE projecting behind right lower wing.
The Front line Companies will light Red flares and wave Watson fans.when called upon to do so by the firing of Very Lights from Aeroplane or when they wish to indicate to Contact Aeroplane the position of the Front line.
13. S.O.S.Signal is a green light fired from a Very Pistol.
14. Officers Commanding C and A Coys are responsible for keeping touch with 2nd Middlesex on Right and 8th Royal Dub.Fus.on left respectively.
15. The Magnetic bearing of the advance is 75 °.

Captain.
Adjutant 7th (S) Bn Royal Irish Rifles.

Copies No 1 & 2 retained.   3 War Diary.
4 A Coy.
5 B Coy.
6 C Coy.
7 D Coy.
8. Quartermaster.
9. Transport Officer.
10. Signalling Officer.
11. Intelligence Officer.
12. Medical Officer.
13. 48th Inf.Bde.
14. Stokes Gun.Officer.
15. M.G.Officer.
16. O.C.8th Dub. Carrying Platoon.
17. 9th Dublins.
18. 2nd Dublins.
19. 2nd Middlesex Regt.
20. R.S.M.

21. Commanding Officer.

SECRET.   7th (S) BN ROYAL IRISH RIFLES.   Copy No...3...

ORDER NO 134.
15th August 1917.

1. The Battalion will parade under cover of hedges ready to march off at 7 p.m. to-day.
2. Order of March. C Coy, D Coy, A Coy, B Coy and Hdqrs.
   Dress. Fighting Order with packs and no haversacks or greatcoats.
   Every man will carry one days ration in addition to his Iron Ration and two full waterbottles. 40 shovels per Coy will be carried. Men carrying shovels will not carry entrenching implements.
3. Head of column will pass MENIN GATE at 8-30 p.m. and will move by "J" Route to assembly positions behind BLACK LINE in D.35.d.
   Companies will form up on tapes laid by R.E. as shown in diagram already issued.
   Markers of the 2nd R.D.Fus. will indicate the Coy Fronts.
4. All Companies will be in position by 3-30 a.m.
5. The importance of absolute silence and absence of lights during the assembly must be impressed on all ranks.
6. Company Commanders will report personally to Battalion Headquarters at D.35.d.4.3. when their Companies are in position.
7. After Battalion has moved off details will proceed to Brigade Detail Camp under Capt W.A.Malone.

                                        Captain.
              Adjutant 7th (S) Bn Royal Irish Rifles.

Copies No 1 & 2 retained.   3 War Diary.
         4 A Coy.
         5 B Coy.
         6 C Coy.
         7 D Coy.
         8 Quartermaster.
         9. Transport Officer.
        10. Signalling Officer.
        11. Intelligence Officer.
        12. 2nd in Command.
        13. 48th Brigade.
        14. Capt W.A.Malone.
        15. R.S.M.
        16. Commanding Officer.
        17. Medical Officer.
        18. Stokes Gun Officer.
        19. M.G.Officer.

SECRET.   7th (S) BN ROYAL IRISH RIFLES.   Copy No......3......

                    O R D E R N O 1 3 5.
In the Field.   Monday 27th August 1917.

---

1. The 16th Division is to relieve the 21st Division in the line in the VI Corps Centre Sector.
2. The 49th Infantry Brigade will move to the Reserve Brigade Area on the 28th August 1917.
3. The 7th Royal Irish Rifles will form up ready to march off at 10-50 am. 28th inst and will proceed to CAMP NO 9 ERVILLERS.
   100 yds distance between companies will be maintained.
4. Advance parties will report to Lieut E.N.Uzielli at Battalion Hdqrs at 8 a.m.
5. All officers valises etc will be stacked at Q.M.Stores by 9-45 a.m.

                                        Captain.
                    Adjutant 7th (S) Bn Royal Irish Rifles.

Copies No 1 & 2 retained.   3 War Diary.
        4 A Coy.   5 B Coy.   6 C Coy.   7 D Coy.
        8. Quartermaster.
        9 Transport Officer.
        10 Signalling Officer.
        11 Second in Command.
        12 R.S.M.
        13 49th Brigade.
        14 Commanding Officer.
        15 Lt. Uzielli

SECRET   AUGUST 27th, 1917   COPY NO......13.

7/8th.(S)Battalion The Royal Irish Fusiliers Order No.21.

::

1. The Battalion will march to the HAMLINCOURT to-morrow 28th inst.
(S.23.c.4.3.)
Battalion will fall in on Battalion Parade Ground at 10.5.a.m.
ready to move off at 10.20.a.m.
Order of March. Drums,H.Qrs.,"D"Coy.,"C"Coy.,"B"Coy.,& "A"Coy.
100 yards interval must be maintained between Companies.
Distance about 5½ miles.

2. KITS.
Company Mess Boxes, Orderly Room Kit and Officers' Kits will be
stacked outside Orderly Room at 9.0.a.m.

3. DRESS. Full marching Order.

4. All Billets must be left clean.

5. Dinners will be cooked on the march and be ready on arrival in the
new Camp.

6. Brigade H.Qrs. will close at ACHIET - LE - PETIT at 11.0.a.m. and will
open at S.33.d.5.5. on arrival there.

7. ADVANCE PARTY.
2/Lieut. C.E.J.NEAT, 4.C.Q.M.Sgts and Sergt.Bird will leave at 7.0.a.m.
28th inst. and proceed to take the new Camp.

8. REVEILLE &c.
Reveille to-morrow will be at 6.0.a.m., Breakfasts 7.0.a.m.

9. ACKNOWLEDGE.

                            2/Lieutenant.
                            A/Adjutant.
         7/8th.(S)Battalion The Royal Irish Fusiliers.

Issued through Signals at 6.15.p.m.

Copy No.1. "A"Coy.	Copy No.7. M.O.
2. "B"Coy.	8. R.S.M.
3. "C"Coy.	9. H.Q.49.Inf.Bde.
4. "D"Coy.	10. Signals.
5. Quartermaster	11. File
6. Transport Officer.	12. Spare

             13 & 14 War Diary.

SECRET   COPY NO....11....

AUGUST 21st. 1917

7/8th.(S)Battalion The Royal Irish Fusiliers Order No.21.
::

1. The Battalion will entrain at BAVINCHOVE STATION at 12.50.p.m. 22nd.inst.and will detrain at MIRAUMONT at 8.50.p.m.on the same day.

2. The Battalion will fall in to pass Starting Point 300 yards S.of Road Junction at Q.15.d.0.5.on road to EECKE by 8.20.a.m. on the 22nd. inst.
   Order Of March.   H.Qrs. "A"Coy., "B"Coy., "C"Coy., & "D"Coy.

3. Transport & Q.M.Stores.
   The Regimental Transport will move off at 7.30.a.m.and should arrive at BAVINCHOVE STATION at 9.50.a.m. 22nd.inst.The Q.M.'& Details should go with the Tranport.

4. The Transport Officer will take with him a complete Marching Out State of the Battalion for information at Entrainment for the R.T.O.

5. KITS.
   Company Mess Boxes and Orderly Room Kit should be stacked outside Q.M.Stores at Battalion H.Qrs to night before 10.0.p.m. Officers' Kits must be stacked outside Q.M.Stores by 6.30.a.m.22nd.inst. One N.C.O.and Storeman per Company will parade at H.Qrs.to morrow at 6.45.a.m.to proceed with packs in Lorry to BAVINCHOVE STATION. 21672 Pte.Sherlock will represent H.Qrs.They will take all their kit with them and be under the Orders of the Q.M.

6. DRESS
   Fighting Order will be worn with Steel Helmets.

7. ROUTE.
   Q.15.c.8.0. -- EECKE--- ST.SYLVESTRE -- P.14.a.5.7. -- LA CHAPELLE -- O.12.d.5.9. -- OXALENE -- BAVINCHOVE.Sheet 27. Approximate distance 7½.Miles.

8. Companies will collect their Packs on arrival at BAVINCHOVE STATION These packs will be arranged in separate dumps for each Coy.& H.Qrs.

9. Billets must be left clean.

10. Horses   There will be no horses for any Officers with the exception of Commanding Officer,Adjutant.& C.O's Groom.

11. RATIONS.   Companies should issue Rations for the 22nd.to the men to night.These will be carried in the Haversack.

12. PICQUETS   The Companies who are entrained at the front and rear of the train should tell off a guard on the Right and Left Side res-pectively to prevent troops leaving train at halts.All doors of covered trucks and carriages on the right hand side of the train when on the main line should be kept closed.

13 Acknowledge

                                    2/Lieut.& A/Adjutant.
                        7/8th.(S)Battalion The Royal Irish Fusiliers

Issued through Signals at 6.0.P.M.21st.inst.

Copy No.1."A"Coy.   Copy.No.7.M.O.
      2. "B"Coy.   8.Sigs.
      3. "C"Coy.   9.R.S.M.
      4. "D"Coy.   10. H.Q.49.Inf.Bde.
      5. Q.M.   11. War Diary.
      6. T.Officer   12. File.
                        13 & 14. Spare.

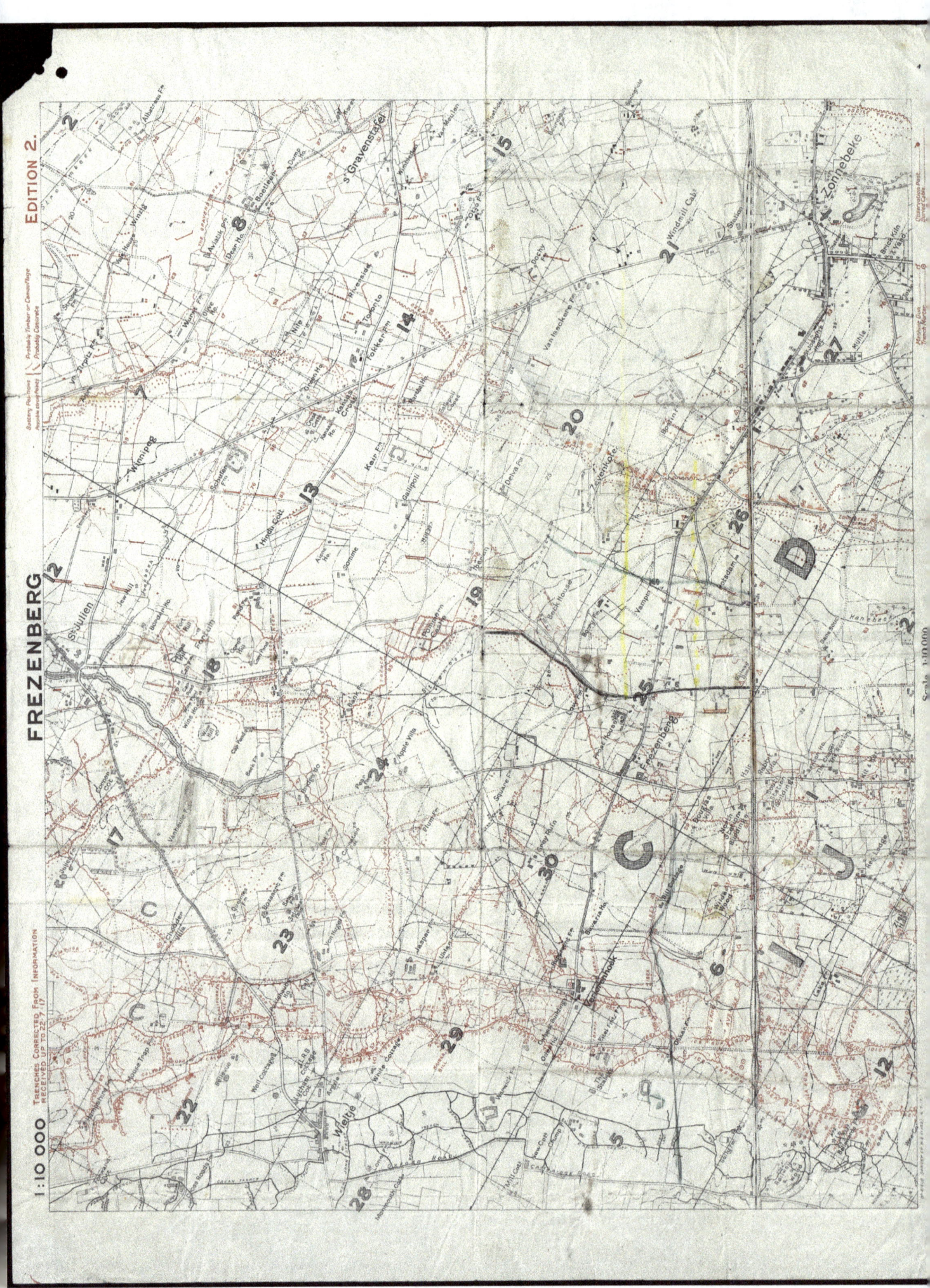

WAR DIARY.

FOR MONTH OF SEPTEMBER, 1917.

VOLUME 22

UNIT:- 7th Batn. R. Irish Rifles

Went to 109" Bde 36 Div October 1917
Absorbed by 2" Bn. 14/11/17.

Vol 22

Army Form C. 2118.

WAR DIARY
or
INTELLIGENCE SUMMARY

(Erase heading not required.)

57C and 51B S.W. 3,000

Place	Date	Hour	Summary of Events and Information	Remarks and references to Appendices
ERVILLERS	1-9-17		The Batt. remained in Div. Reserve.	
"	2-9-17		In Div. Reserve by Tunney being carried out.	A
"	3-9-17		Coy. Cmdrs & C.O. made reconnaissance of new line to be taken over from 48th Inf. Bde. Capt. E. Hope Carson reported off leave. 2nd Lt. Crawford returned from rest Camp. 2nd Lt. H.M. Burcher went to Hospital.	A
TRENCHES	4-9-17		The Batt. relieved the 8th R. Dub. Fus. 48th Inf. Bde. in left subsection in accordance with order No. 136 attacked. Relief was complete at 7.35 p.m. Fine weather. Bn. hunches. Bn. HQrs in shaft 46 of old German tunnel running underneath HINDENBURG LINE.	A
"	5-9-17		Quiet day. Bty. had three men wounded by a trench mortar.	
"	6-9-17		Very quiet. No casualties	A
"	7-9-17		Still quiet. Lt. Col. Francis went on leave.	
"	8-9-17		There was also a quiet day. Nothing unusual occurring	A/6

WAR DIARY
or
INTELLIGENCE SUMMARY.
(Erase heading not required.)

Army Form C. 2118.

Place	Date	Hour	Summary of Events and Information	Remarks and references to Appendices
TRENCHES	9-9-17		Capt Little instructed to report to War Office proceeded to-day. Capt McSorley took over duties of Adjutant	A/6
"	10-9-17		Relieved by 7/8th R.Ir.Fus. in Left sub-section in accordance with Order 137 attached. Relief complete by 10.10 p.m. Went into Bde support with Bn Hd Qrs at T22 D 5.9 7/Lr & M.B. Cyrie MC returned from hospital	A/6
SHEET S7B	Eg 000			
	11-9-17		Capt Turner R.A.M.C. proceeded on leave. Was relieved by Capt Nicholls R.A.M.C. 113R 7d. Ambulance	A/6
	12-9-17		Coys & Bn Hd Qrs preparing dugouts with a view to good winter accommodation & plied carrying	A/6
	13-9-17			
	14-9-17		party of 30 for T.M.B. on 12th and parties of 10 for M/A from Bde each day.	A/A

WAR DIARY or INTELLIGENCE SUMMARY

Army Form C. 2118.

Place	Date	Hour	Summary of Events and Information	Remarks and references to Appendices
TRENCHES	15-9-17		Usual work maintaining and improving trenches. 2/Lt ERNEST COCKBURN KYTE joined the Bn for duty	
	16-9-17		Relieved by 6th R.D. FUSILIERS and moved into Div. Reserve at BELFAST CAMP, ERVILLERS B13 central. 00138 attacked	
ERVILLERS	17-9-17		Baths and cleaning equipment also supplying working parties	
	18-9-17		for Musketry Range, Bayonet fighting Course etc	
	19-9-17		Training of Coys. The Regt. football team played 144 Coy R.E. Won 3 goals nil	
	20-9-17		Lt Col FRANCIS D.S.O. returned from leave	
	21-9-17		MAJOR D REID rejoined for duty supplying working parties. Making improvements in camp	
	22-9-17		MAJOR RIGG went on leave	
	23-9-17		Sunday Church Quarters	
	24-9-17		Bn ceremonial drill	
	25-9-17		Bde ceremonial parade. Bns marching past and advancing in Review order.	

WAR DIARY
or
INTELLIGENCE SUMMARY

Army Form C. 2118.

Place	Date	Hour	Summary of Events and Information	Remarks and references to Appendices
ERVILLERS	26-9-17 to 27-9-17		Coy training. 3 Officers & O.R. from S.I.House attacked for instruction. Baths for men. Capt. G.B.J. Smyth went on leave.	FJB
TRENCHES	28-9-17		Relieved 8th R.D. Fusiliers in the Left Sub section in accordance with attached O.O. No. 39. Relief complete at 5.40 p.m. 2 Lieuts Young, Woulfe & Cochrane joined 4-9th T.M.B. today.	MJH
"	29-9-17		One man in A Coy slightly wounded. Day fairly quiet. A few shells landed close to D Coy H.Q. did damage. A strombos [horn] Bn awarded 19 M.M.'s dated August 17. We had one man killed today but the day was exceptionally quiet for bravery during operations at YPRES in August 17. Enemy dropped a parachute behind our lines with a copy of the Gazette des Ardennes attached. M/G Battery kept for Lt. Col. Ratter of O.C. 1/10 R.Dr. Rifles	MJH MJ/16 MJH MJH MJH
"	30-9-17			

1/10/17

7th (S) BN ROYAL IRISH RIFLES.   Copy No......

ORDER NO 136.

In the Field.   Monday 3rd Sept 1917.

Reference Sheet 31 B.S.W. 1/20,000 and Trench Map.

1. The 49th Inf. Bde. (Less M.G.Company) will relieve the 48th Inf.Bde. (less M.G.Company) in the left Section on the 4th September in accordance with the attached relief table.

2. The 7th Royal Irish Rifles will relieve the 8th R.D.Fus. and 1 Coy 10th R.D.Fus. in the left subsection,(Southern Boundary, will be LUMP LANE inclusive, Northern Boundary, PUG AVENUE.
   A Coy on right from LUMP LANE to SENSEE RIVER.
   B Coy from SENSEE RIVER to KARL LANE (inclusive).
   C Coy from KARL LANE to HORN TRENCH (with posts in front).
   D Coy from HORN TRENCH to PUG AVENUE (with posts in front).
   Battalion Headquarters in SHAFT TRENCH (T.6.b.3.0.)

3. Advance parties consisting of 1 Officer per Company, 1 N.C.O. per platoon, gas N.C.O's, proportion of signallers, and Nos 1 of Lewis Gun teams will meet guides at BDE H.Q. T.21.d.5.9 at 10 a.m. on 4th inst.

4. One guide per platoon, 1 per Coy Hdqrs and 1 for Bn Hdqrs from 8th R.D.Fus will be at Brigade Hdqrs T.21.d.5.9. at 4-30 p.m. 4th inst. Leading Company will march off in time to reach Brigade Hdqrs at 4-30 p.m. This does not apply to A Coy who will arrange independently with Coy of 10th R.D.Fus.
   ORDER OF MARCH. Hdqrs, B, D, C Coys. A Coy will march independently.
   The Master Cook will arrange to take over cooking arrangements for Battalion less A Coy at STALEY BRIDGE.
   Regimental Aid Post will be in Shaft No.46.

5. All movement will be by platoons at 5 minutes interval.

6. All trench stores, documents etc will be taken over on relief. Lists of everything taken over will be sent to Battalion Hdqrs by 4 p.m. 5th inst.

7. Relief complete will be reported to Battalion Headquarters in CODE by wire and also by runner.

8. ACKNOWLEDGE.

                                              Captain.
                              Adjutant 7th (S) Bn Royal Irish Rifles.

Copies No 1 & 2 retained.   3 War Diary.
         4 A Coy 5 B Coy. 6 C Coy   7 D Coy.
         8 Quartermaster.
         9 Transport Officer.
        10. Signalling Officer.
        11. Medical Officer.
        12. R.S.M.
        13. 49th Bde.
        14. 2nd in Command.
        15. Commanding Officer.

SECRET.   7th (S) Battalion Royal Irish Rifles.   Copy No...4.4...

ORDER NO 137.

Reference sheet B. S.W. 1/20,000.   8th Sept 1917.

1. The 7th IRISH RIFLES will be relieved in the Left Subsection by the 7/8th R.Irish FUS. on the 10th inst and on completion of relief will move into positions vacated by 7/8th R.IRISH.FUS.
2. Reliefs will be carried out in accordance with table attached.
3. Advance parties will proceed to take over new positions at 10 a.m. Each advance party will send at least 1 N.C.O. with relieving Coy to act as guide to Coy after relief.
4. Sunken roads and reverse slopes of hills must be taken as much advantage of as possible both during the relief and afterwards.
5. All movement will be by platoons at 5 minutes interval.
6. All work ; defence arrangements, trench stores etc will be handed over. Trench Store lists to be sent to Battalion Headquarters by 10 a.m. 11th inst.
7. Dixies, periscopes and Lewis Gun Magazines will be taken out of the line on relief.
8. Dressing Station will be at Battalion Headquarters.
9. Relief complete will be notified to Battalion Headquarters by wire ; Code word will be "EXCELSIOR". Companies will send 2 runners to Battalion Headquarters at T.2a.d.5.9. when in new position.

H Steele
Captain.
Adjutant 7th (S) Bn Royal Irish Rifles.

Copy No 1 & 2 retained.
3 A Coy. 4 B Coy. 5 C Coy. 6 D Coy. 7. Quartermaster
8 Transport Officer.   9.   7/8th R.I.Fus.   10 R.S.M.
11 40th Inf. Bde.   12. Commanding Officer.
13.Signalling Officer.   14.   War Diary.

Coy of Irish Rifles to be relieved in Front Line.	Coy of Irish Fusiliers relieving in Front Line.	Move to after relief.	Guides.	Remarks.
A.	D.	Positions vacated by D Coy. R.Ir.Fus. (T.23.a.2.2.)	Own arrangements.	Relief to be complete by 7 p.m.
B.	B.	Position vacated by B Coy. R.Ir.Fus. (Posts C 6 to C10).	One guide per platoon 1 for Coy Hdqrs to be at STALEY BRIDGE at 7/30 p.m.	
C.	C.	Position vacated by C Coy. R.Ir.Fus. (T.17.a.4.2.).	ditto.	
D.	A.	Position vacated by A Coy. R.Ir.Fus. (Shaft Trench).	Own arrangements.	Relief to be complete by 6 p.m. NELLY AVENUE can be used up to 5-30 p.m.
Hdqrs	Hdqrs	Headqrs vacated by R.Ir.Fus (T.22.d.5.9).	One guide to be at STALEY BRIDGE at 7/30 p.m.	

SECRET.   7th (S) BN ROYAL IRISH RIFLES.   Copy No...14......

O R D E R   N O   1 3 5.

Reference 5 1 F S.W.1/20,000 and 57 C. N.W. 1/20,000.
16th Sept 1917.

---

1. The 7th IRISH RIFLES will be relieved by the 8th DUBLINS on the 16th inst, and on completion of relief will move into BELFAST CAMP ERVILLERS (B 13 B.1.1.).

2. Reliefs will be carried out in accordance with attached table.

3. Advance parties will report to Lieut E.N.Uzielli at new camp at 12 noon.

4. All movement will be by platoons at 5 minutes interval.

5. All work, defence arrangements, trench stores, etc will be handed over on relief. Box Periscopes will also be handed over and receipts obtained. Lists of stores handed over to be rendered to Battalion Headquarters by 9 a.m. 17th inst.

6. Dixies and Lewis Gun Magazines will not be handed over.

7. Completion of relief will be reported to Battalion Headquarters in code by wire. Code word will be GAZETTE.

8. Relief to be complete by 4 p.m.

9. Transport Officer will make necessary arrangements for transport.

10. Acknowledge.

                                                    Captain.
                A/Adjutant 7th (S) Bn Royal Irish Rifles.

Copies No 1 & 2 retained.
           3 A Coy.
           4 B Coy.
           5 C Coy.
           6 D Coy.
           7 Quartermaster.
           8 Transport Officer.
           9. 49th Bde.
          10. R.S.M.
          11. 8th Dublins.
          12. Commanding Officer.
          13. Medical Officer.
          14. War Diary.

Coy of R.I.R. to be relieved	Coy of R.D.F. relieving.	Move to after relief.	Guides.
A.	A.	BELFAST CAMP ENVILLERS.	To be at RAILWAY CROSSING T.27.a.1.8. at 12-30 p.m.
B.	D.	ditto.	ditto.
C.	B.	ditto.	ditto.
D.	C.	ditto.	2 Guides at STALEY BRIDGE at 2 p.m.
Hdqrs.	Hdqrs.	ditto.	To be at RAILWAY CROSSING T.27.a.1.8. at 12-30 p.m.

SECRET.   Copy No. 15

7th (Service) Battalion Royal Irish Rifles.

OPERATION ORDER NO. 139.

1. The 49th Infantry Brigade (less M.G.Coy) will
   relieve the 48th Infantry Brigade (less M.G.Coy)
   in the Left Section on the 28th Septr.1917, in

2. The 7th R.Irish Rifles will relieve the 8th R.
   Dublin Fusiliers in the Left Sub Section in the
   following order:
   - C Company........on Right.
   - D Company........on Right Centre.
   - A Company........on Left Centre.
   - B Company........on Left.
   - Battn H.Q. in Shaft Trench T.6.B.5.0.

3. Advance Parties of 1 Officer per Coy, 1 N.C.O.
   per Platoon, Gas N.C.O., 1 Signaller and No.1.of
   Lewis Gun Teams will leave at 10.0.a.m.

4. The leading Company will march off at 1.30 p.m.

5. <u>ORDER OF MARCH:</u> D Coy., B Coy., A Coy., H.Qrs.
   C Coy, will march independently.

6. Guides will meet A.B. and D Coys at C.10. at 3.P.pm
   Guide will meet C Coy at St.LEGER at 2.6 p.m.

7. The Master Cook will arrange to take over Cooking
   arrangements for Battn, less C Coy, at STALY BRIDGE.

8. Movement by Platoons at five minutes interval.

9. All Trench Stores, documents, etc, to be taken over
   (Aero photos will NOT be taken over).
   Lists to be sent to Battn. H.Q. by 10.9.a.m.29th inst

10. Completion of Relief to be reported to Bn H.Q. in
    Code and by runner.
    Code Word "WELLINGTON"

Acknowledge.

M J Hartery, Captain,
A/Adjutant 7th (S)/Bn Royal Irish Rifles.

Copy No.1. & 2 retained. 3. A Coy. 4 B Coy. 5 C Coy.
         6 D Coy. 7 Quartermaster. 8 Transport Officer
         9 48th Inf. Bde. 10 Signal Officer. 11.R.S.M.
         12 Intelligence Officer. 13 2nd i/c. 14.M.O.
         15. War Diary. 16 Commanding Officer.

36TH DIVISION
108TH INFY BDE

Attached

7TH BN ROY. IRISH RIF.
OCT - NOV 1917

WAR DIARY
or
INTELLIGENCE SUMMARY

Army Form C. 2118.

7 R I Rif[les]

Place	Date	Hour	Summary of Events and Information	Remarks and references to Appendices
TRENCHES S15SW20,000 S7c+ S5BSW 30,000 + S15SW	1-10-17		During a mist about 8 a.m. a party of 8 of the enemy came close to our line at U17/175 and kept along the SENSÉE river thirty sweeping machine gun fire. An enemy one of C Coys sentry posts they were bombed by the sentry & immediately retired. 1 Cpl. remaining of the day was noticeably quiet. 1 Point Darley was slightly wounded in the hand, but remained at duty.	MR
	1-10-17		At 7 p.m. Capt Malone and 6 O.R. further noticed a rem[nant?] the MERU at the end of STUMP LANE. Plans were immediately made for the capture of the MERU. At 3.45 a.m. next morning 2/Lt McConnell and 16 men of A Coy attacked the it but found the enemy had then vacated it. Ours being held by us	MR
	2-10-17		D Coys Stumper places today. One Lewis Gun team of C Coys had bad luck all twenty wounded by a freak morning burst. Lt & 2 O.R. were killed and 3 wounded	MR
	3-10-17		all C...	MR

WAR DIARY

Army Form C. 2118.

Place	Date	Hour	Summary of Events and Information	Remarks and references to Appendices
TRENCHES	4-10-17		Relieved 10/17th R.S. Fusiliers in accordance with O 140 attached. Completed at 1.15 pm. On completion used in the Battn dispositions were as follows: A Coy T17 a 2 B Coy Stalybridge. C Coy Posts C6 & C10. D Coy T22 a22. HQ T22 d 5.9	App 1
	5-10-17		Troops in support billets comfortable. Snowing English shelters in A. D & HQ position under supervision of R.E. Major Biggs received from	App 16
	6-10-17		Source supply & Sown & follow up fatigue parties 1 NCO + 1 men BB HQ daily. 1 NCO & 10 men Stalybridge for wire on Oakham.	App 6
	7-10-17		Weather cold. 2/Lts J.C.B. RYAN and F.W. HOWROYD from 3rd R.I. Regt joined the battalion for duty	App 6
	8-10-17			
	9-10-17		Continuing snow or wet. Nothing unusual occurred on these days	App 11
ERVILLERS	10-10-17		Relieved by the 8th R Dublin Fusiliers and on relief battalion was billeted in BELFAST CAMP ERVILLERS. Relief was complete at 3.25 p.m. Rein/orders (order no.141) attached.	App 6
	11-10-17		Bath at ERVILLERS & Battn to the O.Y. today, but owing to a	App 6

WAR DIARY
INTELLIGENCE SUMMARY

Army Form C. 2118.

Place	Date	Hour	Summary of Events and Information	Remarks and references to Appendices
ERVILLERS	11-10-17		Location known, they were unable to be used when parties arrived there. Genl HICKIE commanding 16th Division inspected the battalion the afternoon (at 4.0pm) He made a short speech in which he told the men would be disbanded in a few days. Officers and men who desired to remain in the Division to field Arm So the remainder of the Battalion would go to the 36th Division and he amalgamated with the 2nd Bn R.I. Rifles of the Division. He thanked the Bn for the good work it had done in the Division and witnessed.	J.J.K
	12-10-17		As baths at BEUGNATRE were still held on bath hut-low Ltd Lieut Col Franklin D.S.O took 20 or so a 9th of the Bn to HARBONNE. Gas went on leave today. Capt G.B.F. Smyth returned from leave.	J.J.K
	13-10-17		Men remaining in 16th Division joined their respective records today. 88 Other Ranks left the battalion. The remainder in staying in the Division were either on Lieu - on leave, in hospital or attached to...	J.J.K

Army Form C. 2118.

WAR DIARY
or
INTELLIGENCE SUMMARY.

(Erase heading not required.)

SHEET LENS 10000

Instructions regarding War Diaries and Intelligence Summaries are contained in F. S. Regs. Part II. and the Staff Manual respectively. Title pages will be prepared in manuscript.

Place	Date	Hour	Summary of Events and Information	Remarks and references to Appendices
ERVILLERS	13·10·17		Divn. Ord. Bde. Ord. Ord. Advance party of 17th (S.I.R.) R.I. Regt which is taking the Battalion's place in the 19th Bde arrived about midnight.	MJK
"	14·10·17		Bn moved to BAPAUME (minus 6 Officers to join the 36th Divn.) Rested. Officers from ERVILLERS at 11 a.m. and arrived at destination at 1.0 p.m.	MJK
			Following Officers were sent to join units:—	
			Major W.T. Ross 10th R. Dub. Fusiliers	
			Capt. W.S. Maitland 2nd " (do)	
			" Wm. Boyle 7/8th R. I. Fusiliers (do)	MJK
			Lt. A.F. Watkins (do)	
			2/Lt. J.E. Barry 6th Connaught Rangers	
	15·10·17		Moved from BAPAUME to YPRES leaving at 9.30 a.m. during our stay at 1 pm. Arrived in YRES at 3.0 pm were billeted in an ex-Divn HQ. So. W of the men were in tents	MJK

Army Form C. 2118.

WAR DIARY
or
INTELLIGENCE SUMMARY.
(Erase heading not required.)

Place	Date	Hour	Summary of Events and Information	Remarks and references to Appendices
YPRES	16.10.17		Inspected by the G.O.C. 36th Division under which we are now serving. Inspected at 2.0 p.m and marched past after the inspection. Have received that Col Travers D.S.O. had been given command of the 111th Bde 37th Div. He spoke to the Bn on parade and thanked everybody very much for the manner in which they had worked under him. Everybody was pleased to hear the good news	
	17.10.17		The Bn started doing fatigues for C.R.A. supplying 3 companies the remaining coy supplied a fatigue party for the Town Major and one for cleaning up camp. Also a party to avoid Transport Officers to meet temporary horses hire. These fatigues were found daily except on Sundays. Brig. Gen. Travers D.S.O. handed over command of the Bn to Major G. Fos/u.Carlow and left to take over his brigade. Staff a great send off. Those men who were in camp	
	18.10.17			

Army Form C. 2118.

WAR DIARY
or
INTELLIGENCE SUMMARY.
(Erase heading not required.)

Place	Date	Hour	Summary of Events and Information	Remarks and references to Appendices
YPRES	19.10.17		Fatigue parties as usual. We had an inter-company football match nearly every afternoon	
"	20.10.17		Church Parades	
"	21.10.17 to 25.10.17		Working beyond fatigue parties. Started an NCO's training class on the 25th. Capt Ogin went on leave on 22nd.	
"	26.10.17		Very wet day. Played the 2/4 K.O.Y.L.I. in football in a downpour of rain. Won 2 goals to nil.	
"	27.10.17		Major D. Reity transferred to 6/7th Royal Scots Fusiliers left to join his unit today	
"	28.10.17		Church Parades. A coy played 11th KRIR Regts in football. Won 3 to 2	
"	29.10.17		Lieut Bratby rejoined from leave today	

WAR DIARY
or
INTELLIGENCE SUMMARY.

Army Form C. 2118.

Place	Date	Hour	Summary of Events and Information	Remarks and references to Appendices
YTRES	30.10.17		Nothing unusual occurred	G.H.
"	31.10.17		2/Lieut William Jones joined the battalion for duty. Posted to D Coy.	G.H.

GHopeCarson.
Major
O.C. 7th R.I. Rifles

1/11/17

SECRET.   ORDER No. 140   Copy No....15
                              by
                   LIEUT COL E. G. FRANCIS. D.S.O.
                            Commanding
                   7th (Service) Batt. Royal Irish Rifles.
In the Field.   October 2nd, 1916.
Reference: Bde. S.S. 1/30.39.

1. The 7th Royal Irish Rifles will be relieved in the Left Sub
   Sector by the 7/8th Royal Irish Fusiliers on the 4th instant
   and on completion of relief will move into positions vacated
   by the 7/8th Royal Irish Fusiliers.

2. Reliefs will be effected out in accordance with attached Table.

3. Advance parties will proceed to take over at 10.a.m.
   Each party will send at least one N.C.O. back to meet Coy. and
   act as guide after relief.

4. All movement will be by Platoons at five minutes interval.
   Sunken roads and reverse slopes of hills will be taken advantage of as much as possible.

5. All work, Defence Schemes, Trench stores, etc, will be carefully
   handed over, but aeroplane photographs will now be handed over.
   Trench Store lists will reach Batt. H.Q. by 11.a.m. on 5th inst.

6. Dixies will be taken out of the line on relief.
   Completion of relief will be notified in code to Batt. H.Q. by
   wire. Code Word: NELSON.

7. B Coy. will send two runners after relief to C Coy. H.Q. in
   O/s. to form a relay post.

8. Coys (B Coy. excepted) will report by runner to Bn H.Q. when
   in new positions.

9. Acknowledge.

                              M J Hartley Captain.
                              A/Adjutant 7th (S) Bn Royal Irish Rifles.

Copies 1. and 2 retained.   8 Quartermaster
       3 A Coy.   9 Transport Officer
       4 B Coy   12 Regtl Sergt Major
       5 C Coy   13 7/8th R.I. Fusiliers
       6 D Coy   14 Signals
       7 49th Inf Bde.   15 Medical Officer.
                              16 Commanding Officer.
                              17 and 18 War Diary.

SECRET.   Copy No. 14

                    ORDER NO.141
                          by
               Lieut Col. S. G. Francis., D.S.O.
                       Commanding
               7th (Service) Battn Royal Irish Rifles.

                                         In the Field.
                                         October 9th, 1917.
                    ......

1. The Battalion will be relieved by the 8th Royal
   Dublin Fusiliers in Left Support on the 10th inst.
   and on completion of Relief will move into BELFAST
   CAMP, ERVILLERS.

2. B Coy. Royal Dublin Fus will relieve A Coy. R.I.Rifles.
   C Coy   "   "   "   B Coy   "
   D Coy   "   "   "   C Coy   "
   A Coy   "   "   "   D Coy   "

3. Billeting Parties will report at BELFAST CAMP at 12.0.
   NOON.

4. All movement will be by Platoons at five minutes
   interval.

5. All Trench Stores, Defence Schemes, Work in Progress
   and Proposed, etc, will be handed over on relief and
   receipts taken. Lists will be sent to Battalion H.Q.
   by 10.0.a.m. 11th instant.

6. Completion of Relief will be reported to Battalion H.Q
   in code by wire.   Code word: BLIGHTY.

7. Relief to be completed by 4.0.p.m.

8. Transport Officer will make necessary Transport
   arrangements.

9. There will be no teas until Battalion is in Camp.

10. Acknowledge.

                              M J Hartery   Captain.
                       A/Adjutant 7th (S) Bn Royal Irish Rifles.

Copies 1 and 2 retained.   9 Transport Officer.
       3 A Coy.   10 Regtl Sergt Major.
       4 B Coy.   11 8th R. Dublin Fusiliers.
       5 C Coy.   12 Commanding Officer.
       6 D Coy.   13 Signals.
       7 49th Inf.Brigade. 14 and 15 War Diary.
       8 Quartermaster.   16 Medical Officer.

OO.148.   TABLE OF RELIEFS.

Coy. of R.I.Rifles relieved	Coy of R.I.Fus relieve	Move to After Relief.	Guides	Remarks.
A.	B.	Position vacated by D Coy. R.I.Fusiliers (T.17.a.4.8)	Nil	
B.	C.	Position vacated by B Coy R.I.Fusiliers (Shaft Trench)	To be at STALEY BRIDGE at 8.P.M.	
C.	D.	Position vacated by C Coy. R.I.Fusiliers (Posts C.6. to C.10)	ditto.	
D.	A.	Position vacated by A Coy R.I.Fusiliers (T.22.a.3.8.)	To be at QUARRY at 8.P.M.	NELLY & JANET AVES. can be used up to 8.30 P.M.
H.Q.	H.Q.	H.Q. vacated by R.I.F (T.22.c.5.5)	Nil	

WAR DIARY
INTELLIGENCE SUMMARY

Army Form C. 2118.

Sheet: LENS 1/40,000 57c S.W.2 1/40,000 57c S.E 1/40,000

Place	Date	Hour	Summary of Events and Information	Remarks and references to Appendices
YPRES	1-11-17		Busy preparing a roll of the Battalion to hand over to the 2nd R.I.R. when amalgamation takes place.	
	2-11-17			
	3-11-17		All personnel informed. The returned to Ordnance Stores. 2/Lieut F.B. Rytel went on leave.	
	4-11-17			
	5-11-17			
	6-11-17		Nothing beyond the usual working parties, which were supplied daily	
	7-11-17			
	8-11-17		Capt C.A. O'Gier returned from leave today	
	9-11-17		2/Lieut R.J. Thompson rejoined the Bn.	
	10-11-17		Very wet day. 2/Lieut R.J. Thompson went on leave. 2/Lts. McConnell and Beatty interviewed by an R.F.C. Officer with a view.	
	11-11-17		to joining that Corps. Interviews took place at ALBERT. Capt. Wanmason went to hospital. Church parades	
	12-11-17		We were officially notified that the 2nd R.I. Rif. with which the Bn. was being	
	13-11-17		amalgamated would arrive on the 14th inst. and fout up a lot of tents in our camp to accommodate this Bn on it's arrival	

Place	Date	Hour	Summary of Events and Information	Remarks and references to Appendices
YPRES	14-11-17		Lieut. G.S. ROE was detailed to proceed to 36 Division Headqrs to meet the 2nd R. IRISH RIFLES on arrival and conduct them to our camp. Bn arrived at 4.30 pm and conducted to camp where hot coffee was provided for them. LIEUT COL GOODMAN was in command, and took over command of the two battalions on arrival. A conference of all B[att]n commanders of the two battalions was held at 7.0 pm to decide as to how the amalgamation would be carried out. It was decided that Company Commanders would complete the new companies to War Establishment. A Coy of the 2nd B[att]n to be completed from A Coy of the 7th B[att]n, the same applying to the corresponding companies. A Roll being prepared of the new battalion, and of the men over establishment who are being sent to the 36th Divisional Base to be reported to other battalions of the Rifles in the Division.	
"	15-11-17			

WAR DIARY
or
INTELLIGENCE SUMMARY

Army Form C. 2118.

7 R. Inch: Reg'
5 y. C. S.6 / 51924

Place	Date	Hour	Summary of Events and Information	Remarks and references to Appendices
YPRES	15.11.17		having relieved in esq'y 7/R. Inn. Fus. on the north-west of the 1st C. 2nd Bn. of R. Ir. Rgt. in reserve in reg'y B.2. Qui into two battⁿˢ the battalion finally carried to camp in the 14ᵗʰ inst	GHQ
	15.11.17			Major Gen. in hin Kays n[?] 10.7.19. 2ⁿᵈ Rgt.

www.ingramcontent.com/pod-product-compliance
Lightning Source LLC
Chambersburg PA
CBHW081405160426
43193CB00013B/2110